Dred Scott and the Politics of Slavery

LANDMARK LAW CASES

&

AMERICAN SOCIETY

Peter Charles Hoffer
N. E. H. Hull
Series Editors

For a complete list of titles in the series go to www.kansaspress.ku.edu

EARL M. MALTZ

Dred Scott and the Politics of Slavery

UNIVERSITY PRESS OF KANSAS

Published by the University Press of Kansas (Lawrence, Kansas 66045), which was
organized by the Kansas Board of Regents and is operated and funded by Emporia
State University, Fort Hays State University, Kansas State University, Pittsburg State
University, the University of Kansas, and Wichita State University

Library of Congress Cataloging-in-Publication Data

Maltz, Earl M., 1950–
Dred Scott and the politics of slavery / Earl M. Maltz.
p. cm. — (Landmark law cases & American society)
Includes bibliographical references and index.
ISBN 978-0-7006-1502-5 (cloth : alk. paper) — ISBN 978-0-7006-1503-2
(pbk. : alk. paper)   1. Slavery — Law and legislation — United
States — History.   2. Scott, Dred, 1809–1858 — Trials, litigation, etc.
3. Sanford, John F.A., 1806– or 7–1857 — Trials, litigation, etc.
4. Slavery — United States — Legal status of slaves in free states.
5. United States. Supreme Court — History.   I. Title.
KF4545.S5M35   2007
342.7308'7 — dc22   2006035015

British Library Cataloguing-in-Publication Data is available.

Printed in the United States of America

10 9 8 7 6 5 4 3 2 1

The paper used in this publication meets the minimum requirements of the
American National Standard for Permanence of Paper for Printed Library Materials
z39.48-1992.

CONTENTS

There are three U.S. Supreme Court cases that define the boundary between law and politics so sharply and at the same time make such an indelible impact upon our public life that they can be said to have changed the course of our history. Two of those cases, *Brown v. Board of Education* (1954) and *Roe v. Wade* (1973), are familiar to most of us. The third comes from a distant time in both chronological and political terms. It is *Dred Scott v. Sandford* (1857), and it came at the high-water mark of American slavery.

It is hard for modern readers to imagine a nation in which a legal regime of slavery was normal. In half of the country people of color were presumed to be slaves. The disfiguring features of American slavery, including its denial to slaves of all personal and civil legal rights, its thoroughgoing racialism, and its harsh police-state mentality, are gone. Their lasting impress upon our culture remains, however, and that impress makes Earl Maltz's narrative of the case and its impact required reading.

So averse are we to the fundamental assumptions of slaveholding and so disdainful of the arguments that slaveholders offered in justification of their actions, including the notions that people of color were especially suited by nature and Christianity for slavery and that slavery was a positive good for the slaves and their masters, that it is hard for us to understand how typical of its time was the Supreme Court's holding in *Dred Scott*. When Dred Scott sued for his own and his family's freedom on the basis of their sojourn in free states and territories free of slavery under the Missouri Compromise, every federal court that heard the case had little trouble deciding it in favor of slavery.

Maltz's sober, levelheaded, and thoroughly professional account returns us to that time. Although his sympathies clearly lie with the petitioners, he presents the arguments and the thinking of all the parties to the case in a fair and impartial manner. He locates the legal precepts, constitutional texts, and precedents the justices cited in the long conversation held by the nation's leaders over slavery. He tracks the sequence of increasingly complex and strained compromises among pro- and antislave forces and free-soil and slaveholding regions. He demonstrates how political party and sectional influences infiltrated the legal issues, and how in the end the politics of the case contributed to its outcome.

Maltz also provides a thoughtful and incisive reading of the various justices' opinions, for they divided on the grounds for the decision and whether Scott and his family were free. In their substance and style of argument, the opinions captured the entire range of pro- and anti-slavery thinking. In themselves, they thus provide summaries of the legal basis for slavery and the legal foundations for abolitionism.

Many years later, another justice described the Court's handling of *Dred Scott* as a "self-inflicted wound." Maltz traces the impact of the case on Northern and Southern public opinion, demonstrating how a decision meant to resolve once and for all the question of slavery in the territories aggravated sectional animosity and made a civil war more likely. The Thirteenth Amendment to the Constitution effectively overturned *Dred Scott*, but the case remains a vital chapter in our legal history, and one we must master if we are to understand that history.

ACKNOWLEDGMENTS

I am deeply indebted to a number of people for their help in the preparation of this book. Perry Dane, Paul Finkelman, and Allan Stein helped me work out a variety of difficult legal issues. The staff of the library at Rutgers School of Law did their usual exemplary job in dealing with research and reference questions. Our secretarial staff, particularly Celia Hazel and Debbie Carr, also provided invaluable assistance and put up with my general craziness. Finally, Mike Briggs and Peter Hoffer went above and beyond in providing guidance and shepherding the project to its conclusion. And, of course, I would be totally lost without my family.

CHAPTER I

Introduction

The delegates to the Constitutional Convention of 1787 did not come to the city of Philadelphia to discuss the issue of slavery. Their task was to create a greatly strengthened federal government that was better suited than the regime of the Articles of Confederation to protecting and advancing their common interests. The delegates did not have a common interest in the future of slavery; in fact, it was an issue over which they were deeply divided. Thus, not surprisingly, none of the delegates to the convention made any effort to federalize the law of slavery.

Nonetheless, for a variety of reasons, the delegates could not avoid the subject entirely. Indeed, they dealt explicitly with a number of issues related to slavery. The Constitution that they produced speaks directly to the role of slaves in determining the states' level of taxation and basis of representation in the House of Representatives, the status of fugitive slaves, and the power of Congress to regulate the international slave trade. In addition, a number of commentators have argued that a variety of other provisions in the Constitution were at least indirectly related to the protection of slavery. The Anti-Federalists attacked a variety of the slavery-related clauses during the ratification process but were unsuccessful in convincing the delegates to the state ratification conventions that these provisions provided sufficient justification for rejecting the new Constitution.

However, as the nation expanded geographically, an issue that was not mentioned in the Constitution came to the fore and ultimately threatened the very existence of the Union itself. The United States purchased the Louisiana Territory from France in 1803 and then in rapid succession acquired Texas, the Oregon Territory, and the Mexican Cession in the 1840s. Bitter sectional disputes arose over the question of whether slavery would be allowed in each of the newly acquired territories. Many Northerners objected on principle to the spread of slavery. Conversely, Southerners contended that banning slavery branded the slaveholders as inferiors rather than equal partners in the Union. Representatives from both sides also realized that the decisions on slavery in the territories could have profound implications for the balance of power within the institutions of the federal government.

The conflict over slavery in the Louisiana Territory was settled by the Missouri Compromise of 1820. Congress was also able to definitively resolve the fate of slavery in Texas and Oregon, albeit with more lasting bitterness among those political leaders who felt they had been defeated. The dispute over the Mexican Cession, however, permanently destabilized the political coalitions that had helped to dampen sectional tensions. Initially, many hoped that the Compromise of 1850 had permanently removed the issue of slavery in the territories from the national political agenda. However, far from being a permanent solution, the measures of 1850 proved to be simply a prelude to the repeal of the Missouri Compromise by the Kansas-Nebraska Act of 1854, the explosion of violence between proslavery and antislavery forces in Kansas, and the reorganization of national politics along strictly sectional lines.

It was against this background that *Dred Scott v. Sandford* came to the Supreme Court in 1856. The case began as a simple lawsuit in state court seeking to win freedom for a family of African Americans in the slave state of Missouri. After being rebuffed by the Missouri Supreme Court, the members of the Scott family turned to the federal courts. When their case came to the U.S. Supreme Court, the justices were initially inclined to reach a decision on grounds that would not have implicated the sectional conflict. After *Dred Scott* was reargued, however, the Southern justices — a majority on the Court — boldly decided to use the case as a vehicle to constitutionalize the position of the slave states on the issue of slavery in the territories. By doing so, they hoped to finally settle the controversy in favor of the South and to devitalize the newly formed Republican Party.

However, the Southern justices failed in this effort. Far from resolving the sectional conflict, the *Dred Scott* decision further exacerbated the tensions between North and South. The Republican Party seized on the decision as evidence of a conspiracy to nationalize slavery and used that charge to good effect in the crucial election campaign of 1860. Moreover, the doctrines established by the case did not long survive. After the secession of the Southern states and the Union victory in the Civil War, the adoption of the Thirteenth and Fourteenth Amendments to the Constitution definitively rejected the holdings of the Court. Ultimately, then, this book is the story of a colossal judicial failure.

The Politics of Slavery, 1785–1842

From the time that the nation was founded, white Americans were deeply divided over the institution of slavery. Many prominent citizens in both the North and the South believed that slavery was morally wrong and worked to persuade state governments to outlaw the "peculiar institution." Some also pressed for federal legislation that was unfriendly to slavery. However, prior to the Civil War, no mainstream politician seriously suggested that the federal government should take direct action to outlaw slavery in states where slavery was permitted under state law.

Nonetheless, issues related to slavery periodically roiled the American political landscape in the period from 1785 to 1842. These issues arose in a wide variety of different contexts and often created intense sectional tensions. Three of these struggles stand out for their long-range implications. The first was the adoption of the Northwest Ordinance. The second was the debate in the Constitutional Convention over the basis of representation in the House of Representatives. The third was the effort to provide for the abolition of slavery in Missouri as a condition of its admission to the Union.

The Northwest Ordinance, adopted under the regime of the Articles of Confederation, provided the framework for the establishment of territorial governments for the land between the Allegheny Mountains and the Mississippi River that had been ceded to the federal government by a number of states. The issue of slavery was addressed in March 1784, early in the drafting process, when a committee chaired by Thomas Jefferson proposed a plan for the temporary government of the region that included a provision that would have outlawed slavery in the territory after the year 1800. Richard Dobbs Spaight of North Carolina challenged this provision, and in a vote taken on April 19, Jefferson's proposal narrowly failed to gain the requisite support in the Continental Congress. The following year, Rufus King of New York failed in his effort to have a similar measure adopted. Finally, on July 13, 1787, Congress united around a motion by Nathan Dane of Massachusetts to add a prohibition on slavery to the Northwest Ordinance, the comprehensive plan that provided for the organization of the territory north of the Ohio River. By contrast, although patterned generally on the Northwest Ordinance, the Southwest Ordinance of 1790 pointedly omitted the provision outlawing slavery. All of the relevant parties seem to have assumed that slavery would be permitted in the absence of such a prohibition. Thus, by its silence, Congress implicitly sanctioned the existence of slavery in the federal domain south of the Ohio River.

This decision simply reflected the political realities of the situation. In practical terms, Congress lacked the ability to effectively prevent the spread of slavery to the southwestern territories. Federal power over these territories was dependent upon effective acts of cession by Virginia, North Carolina, and South Carolina, and these states simply would not have acquiesced in the prohibition of slavery in their former lands. Indeed, the only practical consequence of Jefferson's near-successful effort in 1784 was the decision of the North Carolina legislature to repeal its act of cession. When North Carolina adopted a new act of cession in 1789, the act's terms specifically prohibited Congress from outlawing slavery in the ceded territory. Given this reality, even the most antislavery members of Congress had little choice but to ultimately accept the continuation of the institution of slavery in the territory ceded by the Southern states.

Against this background, the only real question is why the Southern delegates acquiesced in the antislavery provision of the Northwest Ordinance in 1787. Southerners clearly had the political power to block the adoption of the provision if they had so wished. Half of the eight state delegations that were present to vote on Dane's proposal were from the South, as were a majority of the individual delegates and the presiding officer. Nonetheless, the prohibition on slavery in the Northwest passed without open dissent.

Southern acquiescence can be traced to the confluence of a variety of factors. In the late eighteenth century, the division between free states and slave states was less important politically than the division between the interests of the South, whose economy was dependent entirely on agriculture, and those of the Northeast, where mercantile interests were of greater importance. Even without slavery, Southerners saw potential allies in the Northwest, where farmers would be the dominant economic and political force. Moreover, some Southerners believed that by outlawing slavery north of the Ohio River, they could prevent competition in the production of tobacco and indigo. Given these perceptions, Southern delegates were willing to sacrifice slavery in order to facilitate the organization of the Northwest — particularly since the prohibition on slavery was linked with a fugitive slave clause, the first of its kind in the United States.

However, the adoption of the Northwest Ordinance ultimately proved to be a crucial victory for the anti-Southern forces. Subsequent events demonstrated conclusively that, without direct federal intervention, slavery would have taken hold in virtually the entire area, leaving free states an isolated and powerless minority in any sectional struggle. Admittedly, the ultimate extinction of slavery in the Northwest did not occur as quickly or as cleanly as some had hoped. In particular, the state constitution under which Illinois was admitted as a state in 1819 contained a number of provisions that rankled antislavery politicians. But when political divisions were ultimately drawn along sectional lines in the late antebellum era, Ohio, Indiana, and Illinois became important bulwarks of Northern political power.

Article I, Section 3, paragraph 3 of the Constitution, which provides that three-fifths of the number of slaves in a state should be counted in the basis of representation of that state in the House of Representatives, was the product of a far more contentious dynamic. From the beginning of the Constitutional Convention, the four southernmost states were allied with the two largest nonslave states — Massachusetts and Pennsylvania — in supporting the concept that representation in a new federal legislature should be proportional rather than divided equally among the states. By contrast, the advocates of proportional representation divided along sectional lines on the question of how slaves should be counted in the process of determining representation. Pierce Butler and Charles Cotesworth Pinckney of South Carolina argued that slaves should be counted equally with free persons in any population-based system of representation; however, this position was supported only by South Carolina, Georgia, and Delaware. Eldridge Gerry of Massachusetts countered that "blacks are property, are used to the southward as horses and cattle to the northward; and why should their representation be increased to the southward on account of the number of slaves, than horses or oxen to the north." This view was apparently shared by majorities in the delegations from Massachusetts and Pennsylvania. Nonetheless, on July 12, the convention adopted the three-fifths compromise for both representation and direct taxes, and the same provisions were included in the final version of the Constitution.

Whatever its merits in the abstract, the three-fifths clause became an important issue in the ratification debates. Not surprisingly, the complexity of the considerations that led to the adoption of the compromise were often obscured in these debates. Northern Anti-Federalists railed against what they saw as the unfairness of giving any weight to slaves in the basis of representation, whereas James Madison defended the scheme as a plausible accommodation to the needs of the South. Nor did the controversy end with ratification itself; Northern protests against the three-fifths clause did not end until the adoption of the Thirteenth Amendment after the Civil War. The disputed election of 1800 added considerable impetus to these protests.

The basic facts of that election can be described fairly easily. The contest between the Republican candidates, Thomas Jefferson of Virginia and Aaron Burr of New York, and their Federalist counterparts, John Adams of Massachusetts and Charles Cotesworth Pinckney of South Carolina, was decided by the electoral college, in which the representation of each state was determined by adding the number of representatives it sent to the House of Representatives to the number of its senators. Jefferson's ticket received 73 electoral votes, whereas Adams's received only 65. However, Jefferson won an overwhelming majority of the electoral votes from the Southern states. If slaves had not been counted in the basis of representation in the House of Representatives, the number of electoral votes coming from these states would have been correspondingly reduced. Most observers have concluded that such a system would have left Adams with 63 votes to Jefferson's 61. Thus, although the makeup of the electoral college reflected other complexities as well, in a very real sense the three-fifths compromise was crucial to the outcome of the election.

Against this background, New England Federalists in particular reacted angrily to Jefferson's victory. They complained vociferously about the perceived unfairness of the result of the election and referred derisively to Jefferson as the "Negro president" because of the role played in his victory by the three-fifths clause. Bitterness over the election lingered and would be an important factor less than two decades later when the controversy over slavery in the territories reemerged with an explosive force that threatened to blow the Union apart.

The purchase of Louisiana from France set the stage for the confrontation. The acquisition was strongly opposed by some Northern Federalists who feared that the citizens of the states that would ultimately be formed from the vast, newly acquired territory would be allies of the agrarian Republicans and would leave Federalists hopelessly outnumbered in the federal government. The essence of their objection was clearly expressed seven years later by Rep. Josiah Quincy of Massachusetts. Opposing the admission of Louisiana to statehood, Quincy declared that "when you throw the weight of Louisiana into the scale, you destroy the political equipoise contemplated at the time of forming the contract." In such a case, he argued, the states whose power was proportionately diminished would be entirely justified in leaving the Union.

Once again, however, the major problem in the minds of the New Englanders was not that slave states per se would dominate the government. Instead, Quincy and his allies feared that agrarian politicians more generally would use their control of the lawmaking apparatus to adopt policies unfavorable to the mercantile interests that were more prominent in New England. Indeed, men such as Quincy feared the influence of Westerners at least as much as that of slaveholders from the original Southern states. Thus, the staunch Massachusetts Federalist Timothy Pickering proposed to split the nation between the original thirteen states and the western states, and Quincy raised the specter of "Representatives from the Red River and Missouri pouring themselves upon us and . . . managing the concerns of a seaboard fifteen hundred miles at least from their residence." Nonetheless, the three-fifths compromise played an important role in the thinking of those who opposed the Louisiana Purchase. For example, Quincy suggested that New Englanders would not have approved any representation based on slaves if they had believed that the agrarian forces would be further strengthened by the acquisition of lands west of the Mississippi River.

{ *Chapter 2* }

Despite such concerns, those who opposed the Louisiana Purchase outright formed only a small minority. When the Senate was presented with the treaty with France in 1803, only five senators registered their opposition. However, in 1804 the process of establishing a government for the newly acquired territory revealed more clearly the potential for conflict in the future. On January 30, Sen. James Hillhouse of New York proposed a gradual emancipation measure that would have applied to the entire Louisiana Purchase. Hillhouse was supported by a large majority of Northern senators. His proposal was defeated only because a handful of Northerners joined a united South to form a 17-11 majority.

Northern opposition to the addition of new slave states came more powerfully to the fore in early 1819, after the territorial legislature of Missouri petitioned Congress to be allowed to adopt a constitution and form a state government. On February 13, the House of Representatives began consideration of an enabling act designed to grant the petition. Six days later Rep. James Tallmadge Jr. of New York moved to amend the enabling act to prohibit further introduction of slaves into Missouri and to gradually emancipate all slaves held there at the time. The introduction of the Tallmadge amendment set in motion a ferocious political conflict that would not be finally resolved until more than two years later.

Both sides recognized that the struggle over the Tallmadge amendment had implications that reached far beyond the admission of Missouri itself. All seemed to agree that in the absence of affirmative congressional action forbidding slavery or requiring emancipation, settlers would be allowed to hold slaves throughout the Louisiana Purchase and that all of the states eventually formed from that territory would allow slavery. Thus, Rep. John W. Taylor of New York, who because of Tallmadge's absence initially led the antislavery forces in the debate, declared that "our votes [on the Tallmadge amendment] will determine whether the high destinies of this region . . . shall be fulfilled, or whether we shall defeat them by permitting slavery, with all its baleful consequences, to inherit the land."

Without question, the position of Tallmadge, Taylor, and many other representatives from nonslave states was informed in large measure by moral objections to slavery. The previous year Tallmadge had attracted 34 votes in an unsuccessful effort to prevent the admission of the state of Illinois on the ground that its state constitution did not sufficiently conform to the prohibition on slavery in the Northwest Ordinance. Similarly, in opening the debate over Missouri, Taylor noted that white Southerners themselves often described slavery as an immoral institution forced upon them by their ancestors, and that its continued existence was justified only by practical exigencies. He argued that, under this view, there could be no defensible justification for spreading slavery beyond the states in which it currently existed. Southerners such as Speaker Henry Clay of Kentucky and Rep. Philip P. Barbour of Virginia responded by denying that the admission of Missouri as a slave state would increase the total number of slaves in the United States and vigorously asserting the "diffusion" theory, which held that slaves would be happier and better fed if spread throughout the West rather than being crowded together in the Southern states east of the Mississippi.

In addition to moral concerns, political considerations figured prominently in the calculations of Tallmadge and his allies. In 1819 national politics was totally dominated by the Jeffersonian Republicans, who in turn were led by the members of the Virginia dynasty and its Southern allies. Federalists such as Sen. Rufus King of New York viewed slavery as a potential wedge issue that could be used to force the reorganization of national politics along sectional lines. In addition, some Northern Republicans, especially the followers of Governor DeWitt Clinton of New York, resented what they saw as disproportionate Southern influence in the party and hoped to reduce that influence in party councils. Other supporters of the Tallmadge amendment expressed alarm at the possibility that admitting Missouri as a slave state would unduly enhance the power of the South more generally. Thus, Republican Sen. Jonathan Roberts of Pennsylvania complained that unless Congress acted to require emancipation, the admission of Missouri would "benefit . . . the slaveholding interest, pecuniarily and economically. The scale of political power will preponderate in favor of the slaveholding States."

Against this background, Northerners often linked their opposition to slavery in Missouri to the three-fifths compromise. Rufus King launched a full-bore attack on the fairness of including slaves in the basis of representation. Similarly, describing the three-fifths clause as "an important benefit yielded to the slaveholding States, as one of the mutual sacrifices for the Union," he argued that extending its impact to the states created from the Louisiana Purchase would be "unjust in its operations, unequal in its results, and a violation of its original intentions."

The supporters of the Tallmadge amendment at times punctuated their arguments with fiery assaults on the basic structure of Southern society. Taylor, for example, declared that "no monuments are necessary to mark the boundary [between Pennsylvania and Maryland]; that it is easily traced by following the dividing lines between farms highly cultivated and plantations open to the common and overrun with weeds; between stone barns and stone bridges on one side, and stalk cribs and no bridges on the other." Republican Rep. Timothy Fuller of Massachusetts launched an even more vigorous assault on the Southern political system. Fuller disclaimed any intention of interfering with slavery in the original states. At the same time, notwithstanding the fact that slavery was legal in almost all the states at the time that the Constitution was drafted, Fuller contended that slaveholding societies violated the principles of the Declaration of Independence and that the governments in the slave states were not "republican" in form, as required by the guaranty clause of Article IV, Section 4 of the Constitution. Fuller asserted that "the States then holding slaves are permitted, from the necessity of the case and for the sake of Union, to exclude the Republican principle so far, and only so far, as to retain their slaves in servitude."

Southerners attacked the restrictionists from a variety of different perspectives. At times they emphasized the practical difficulties that might be involved in an effort to force Missourians to abandon slavery. Many observers believed that armed federal intervention would be required, and that resistance in Missouri would be supported by the slave states even in the face of contrary action by Congress. As John Tyler of Virginia suggested, it was unreasonable to believe "that Southern bayonets would be plunged into Southern hearts." Others believed that Missourians would simply create their own independent state rather than entering the Union with the restrictions that would have been imposed by the Tallmadge amendment.

However, the core of the antirestrictionist argument was that the Tallmadge amendment violated both the rights of Southerners who wished to emigrate to Missouri with their slaves and those of the people of Missouri, who, it was argued, should have the authority to decide for themselves whether or not to allow slavery in their nascent state. Antirestrictionists often sought to imbue such concerns with a constitutional status. For example, in his initial assault on the amendment, Rep. Philip Barbour of Virginia rejected the claim that Congress had plenary authority to set conditions for the admission of new states. Instead, he contended that new states must be admitted on an equal footing with existing states, and that Congress could not deny them the fundamental sovereign right of deciding whether or not to permit slavery. Similarly, Sen. Freeman Walker of Georgia asserted:

> Whether slavery is an evil or not is a matter for the people of Missouri to determine for themselves, and not Congress for them.... Shall we take from them the right of judging for themselves upon a subject so intimately connected with their welfare? Will those who contend so bitterly against the slavery of the blacks make slaves of the white people of Missouri and rivet chains about their necks? . . . Such a course of conduct might do well for a despot of Europe . . . But for the meek-eyed sons of a Republic to attempt such a thing . . . has excited my astonishment and regret.

Against this background, the Union itself seemed in danger in 1819 and 1820. Rep. Thomas W. Cobb of Virginia warned that the Tallmadge proposal had "kindled a fire which all the waters of the ocean cannot put out, which seas of blood can only extinguish," and John Scott, the territorial delegate from Missouri, asserted that the antislavery proposal was "big with the fate of Caesar and Rome." Tallmadge retorted that "if a dissolution of the Union must take place, let it be so! If civil war . . . must come, I can only say, let it come!"

Given such rhetoric, it should not be surprising that the Tallmadge amendment divided both houses of Congress along sectional lines. The first votes came in 1819. In the House of Representatives, where the representatives of the nonslave states held a clear majority, the proposal to ban slavery in Missouri passed by a vote of 87-76. Only one slave-state representative supported the proposal, and only ten congressmen from the free states voted against it. In the Senate, the balance of power was different. Although the upper house was formally divided equally between the representatives of the free states and those from slave states, both of the senators from Illinois were reliable supporters of the Southern position who themselves owned either slaves or indentured servants. With the South in effective control, the Senate voted 22-16 to strike the prohibition on slavery from the Missouri bill. Neither chamber would recede from its position in 1819, and the Fifteenth Congress adjourned without resolving the issue.

At the same time that Congress was considering the enabling act for Missouri, it was also in the process of establishing a territorial government for Arkansas. In the House of Representatives, John Taylor introduced a provision banning slavery from the territory. Because no question of statehood was involved, some representatives believed that this proposal presented fewer constitutional difficulties than the effort to restrict slavery in Missouri. However, Rep. Felix Walker of North Carolina insisted that "we have no legitimate authority to legislate on the property of citizens, only to levy taxes." Although the proposal to ban slavery from the Arkansas Territory failed on a tie vote, on February 18, 1819, the House voted 75-73 to require the emancipation of all slaves born in Arkansas when they reached the age of twenty-five. The following day, however, the House reversed itself, deleting the gradual emancipation provision by a vote of 89-87.

The critical vote was cast by Rep. Ezekiel Whitman of Massachusetts — the only Northerner who voted against requiring gradual emancipation in Arkansas after having supported a similar requirement for Missouri. Echoing a suggestion first made by Rep. Louis McLane of Delaware, Whitman relied on considerations of geography to justify his position in the controversy over Arkansas. Although deploring the idea of sectional division, he observed that the basic principle had already been established by the Northwest and Southwest Ordinances. Since the territorial boundaries of Missouri were almost entirely north of the Ohio River, Whitman believed that it should be a free state; since Arkansas was south of that line, he was willing to accept slavery there.

Even Tallmadge was willing to make some concessions to the realities of geography. For example, he made no objection to the admission of Alabama as a slave state in 1820, having observed during the debate over Missouri that "surrounded as [Alabama] was by slave-holding States, with only imaginary lines of division, the intercourse between slaves and free blacks could not be prevented, and a *servile* war might be the result." Against this background, a geographical line provided the most promising basis for the resolution of the controversy over the restriction of slavery in Missouri itself.

When the Sixteenth Congress convened in late 1819, the addition of Maine to the equation provided the impetus for the settlement of the Missouri question. In June 1819, the Massachusetts state legislature had agreed to allow the portion of the state that is now Maine to seek admission to the Union as a separate state. However, the statute provided that the permission to separate would expire if Maine was not admitted prior to March 4, 1820. On January 3, 1820, the House of Representatives passed a bill granting a petition to admit Maine to the Union.

In the Senate, the supporters of admission for Missouri without the restriction on slavery, their numbers fortified by the two senators from the newly admitted state of Alabama, seized on the Maine bill as an opportunity to break the impasse. On December 30, 1819, Rep. Henry Clay of Kentucky, the Speaker of the House, announced that Southerners would not acquiesce in the admission of Maine unless Missouri was admitted as a slave state. This maneuver drew inferential support from the already-established tradition of balancing free-state and slave-state admissions in order not to upset the balance of power in the Senate — a practice that had been followed for each new state that had been admitted after the original thirteen states had ratified the Constitution.

On February 16, 1820, by a vote of 23-21, the Senate officially linked the admission of Maine and Missouri in a single bill that would have admitted both states without restrictions. In an attempt to placate the North, the Senate then overwhelmingly adopted a proposal by Sen. Jesse B. Thomas of Illinois that barred further introduction of slavery into the area of the Louisiana Purchase north of 36 degrees, 30 minutes of latitude — the southern border of Missouri. At first the House of Representatives refused to accept this package. However, on March 1, by a vote of 90-87, the House agreed to accept a conference committee report that allowed Missouri to form a government without outlawing slavery. The margin of victory was provided by fourteen Northerners, ten of whom openly supported the removal of the antislavery proviso and four of whom simply absented themselves from the crucial vote.

Even at this point, many Northerners refused to concede defeat on the issue of the admission of Missouri. The passage of the compromise of 1820 did not actually admit Missouri to statehood. Rather, the bill simply authorized Missourians to draft a constitution and form a state government without requiring emancipation. On November 16, 1820, Missouri formally requested admission, submitting a state constitution that included a provision that forbade free blacks and mulattoes from entering the state. Since free blacks were viewed as citizens in a number of Northern states, some Northerners argued that this provision violated the comity clause of the Constitution, which provides that "the citizens of each State shall be entitled to all privileges and immunities of citizens in the several states." The Senate responded to this difficulty by adding a clause to the admitting resolution providing that "nothing herein contained shall be so construed as to give the assent of Congress to any provision in the constitution of Missouri, if any such there be, which contravenes the [comity clause]." However, with Maine now safely admitted, many Northerners in the House of Representatives seized on the exclusion of blacks as justification for refusing to admit Missouri. On December 13, 1820, the House voted against admission by a vote of 93-79. Only five Northerners supported the admitting resolution.

Southerners were outraged by what they saw as a breach of faith by their Northern colleagues. Only hours after the vote, Rep. Francis Jones of Tennessee wrote to a friend, "I am sorry to tell you, that in my opinion, in fact the Union is almost dissolved." Later, Rep. Benjamin Hardin of Kentucky warned that "gentlemen think that if Missouri falls, she will fall alone; but, sir, I will go with her, and so will her sister states, who have blood and treasure." Faced with such sentiments, Henry Clay once again worked furiously to craft a compromise. The Senate resolution was referred to a select committee, which on February 10 proposed that Missouri be admitted without further congressional action if the territorial legislature assented to "the fundamental condition that the said State shall never pass any law preventing any description of persons from coming to and settling in the said State, who now or hereafter may become citizens of any of the States of this Union." Rep. Rollin C. Mallary of Vermont promptly moved to amend the committee resolution to require Missouri to abolish slavery. Although the amendment was beaten back, it received the support of nearly two-thirds of the representatives from the Northern states. When the committee proposal itself was put to a vote, it received the support of a handful of Northern representatives. Nonetheless, the proposal was defeated 83-80 because three Southern congressmen refused to consent to *any* restrictions on Missouri.

Once again the two Houses were deadlocked. At Clay's urging, on February 22 the House of Representatives elected a committee of twenty-three members to meet with seven of their counterparts from the Senate in a last-ditch effort to reach an accommodation. The committee approved a resolution drafted by Clay himself. The resolution provided for the automatic admission of Missouri once the territorial legislature had agreed that the exclusion clause of the Missouri constitution "shall never be construed to authorize the passage of any law, and no law shall be passed in conformity thereto, by which any citizen of either of the States in this Union shall be excluded from the enjoyment of the privileges and immunities to which such citizen is entitled under the Constitution of the United States." In practical terms, this language left the fate of the state constitutional provision in the hands of the courts. On February 26 this resolution passed the House of Representatives by a vote of 87-81, with eighteen Northerners joining a united South to form the majority. The compromise easily passed the Senate on February 28, bringing the crisis over the admission of Missouri to an end.

However one evaluates the substantive merits of the Missouri Compromise, one point is clear: Southerners in Congress were far more willing than their Northern counterparts to countenance a compromise solution. In both the House of Representatives and the Senate, a majority of the representatives of the slave states voted for the Thomas proviso, which barred slavery north of 36 degrees, 30 minutes. By contrast, from the moment James Tallmadge introduced the first antislavery proposal, Northerners in Congress overwhelmingly rejected *any* meaningful compromise on the issue of slavery. Even when the issue of Missouri was linked to the simultaneous admission of Maine and the Thomas proviso, fewer than 19 percent of Northern senators and 14 percent of Northern members of the House of Representatives were willing to admit Missouri without requiring emancipation. Further, Northern opposition was not based primarily on the geographical position of Missouri. To be sure, even Northerners understood that because the Alabama Territory was completely surrounded by states in which slavery was legal, requiring emancipation there was impractical. However, the distribution of support on the final vote to admit Missouri in 1820 was almost precisely the same as the pattern of votes on the measures designed to ban slavery in the Arkansas Territory, which lay entirely south of the Ohio river.

The voting pattern in Congress mirrored widespread dissatisfaction with the compromise in the North generally. To be sure, some Democratic newspapers in the free states hailed what they saw as the defeat of a Federalist political maneuver. However, Theodore Dwight of New York labeled the compromise "a mere farce" and declared that "the Slave States will henceforth maintain the perpetual ascendancy in the national councils, and the Free States, with numbers enough to assert and support all their right and privileges, have voluntarily surrendered them." Similarly, while conceding that "something has been gained in the exclusion of Slavery from the territories," the *Sentinel* of Keene, New Hampshire, complained, "Still we have suffered a disgraceful defeat. We had the power to prevent the *black torrent* from rolling one inch farther." These attitudes were reflected in the returns from the elections of 1820, as only five of the eighteen Northern congressmen who ultimately refused to support restriction in Missouri were returned to office.

Opinion in the slave states was also divided. Some agreed with the assessment of the Charleston *Patriot*, which lauded "that spirit of diffusive patriotism that takes in the welfare of the Union, in opposition to the strength of local attachments." At the same time, the protracted dispute left other Southerners with the belief that they had good reason to question their long-term prospects in the Union. The rhetoric of Northern representatives revealed a deep-seated hostility toward the fundamental institutions of the South. Moreover, the refusal of the vast majority of Northerners to consider any accommodation on the issue of slavery suggested a determination to act on that hostility if similar issues were again presented to Congress. In addition, the dynamic of the controversy clearly revealed limitations in the ability of the Southern states to resist Northern pressure. The representatives of the slave states were outnumbered in the House of Representatives and held precisely half of the seats in the Senate. The slightest change in the balance of power in the Senate would therefore leave the Southern states without the means to defend themselves and their interests within the existing structure. These factors led Thomas Jefferson to view the crisis over Missouri as a "firebell in the night" that had threatened to be the "[death] knell of the Union"; the resolution of the crisis might well prove to be a "reprieve only, and not a final sentence."

Nonetheless, for a time it seemed that the settlement of the Missouri question had at least removed the primary danger to the basic fabric of the Union, although disputes over slavery might occasionally raise sectional tensions. Moreover, the emergence of the second party system created mechanisms that encouraged cooperation between North and South. Martin Van Buren of New York consciously designed the Democratic Party as a national institution to counteract the forces of sectionalism, and by 1840 Henry Clay's Whig Party had emerged as an equally bisectional alternative. Although a substantial number of the Northern members of Congress continued to resist the admission of any new slave states, many others viewed the events of 1819 through 1821 as providing a workable basis for compromise. Thus, in 1836 the admission of Michigan as a free state was paired with that of Arkansas as a slave state. In 1844 Iowa and Florida were similarly joined, once again preserving sectional balance in the Senate.

To be sure, the reemergence of conflict between North and South over slavery-related issues always remained a real possibility. Mainstream elements of both parties were harried by sectional extremists, and accusations of sectional disloyalty were a staple of political campaigns throughout the antebellum era. Occasionally the tensions would bubble to the surface in Congress itself: In the period from 1836 to 1844, the recurrent struggles over the receipt of petitions advocating the abolition of slavery in the District of Columbia were perhaps the most prominent examples. Nonetheless, both parties were dominated by actors who were committed, at least in general terms, to the maintenance of sectional peace. The same impulse was reflected in the slavery-related decisions of the Supreme Court from 1825 to 1842.

CHAPTER 3

The Supreme Court and Slavery, 1825–1842

The Supreme Court played little role in the national debate over slavery during the early years of the nineteenth century. Although the Court was faced with a variety of cases related to slavery during this period, the issues presented were generally prosaic, and their resolution received little national attention. However, beginning in 1841 the Court was faced with three cases in rapid succession, each of which had potentially significant implications for the sectional conflict.

The first of these cases was *Groves v. Slaughter. Groves* arose from an ordinary action to recover on a promissory note for seven thousand dollars that had been given in partial payment for a group of slaves brought into the state of Mississippi for sale in 1836. The suit revolved around a provision of the Mississippi constitution of 1832 that prohibited the introduction of slaves from other states as merchandise or for sale. This provision had apparently been added to the state constitution because of concerns about the outflow of funds to other states, the possibility that the importation of slaves would depress the value of slaves already held in Mississippi, and the fear that slaves were being "sold south" to Mississippi because they were troublemakers. The holder of the note argued that the Mississippi provision violated the federal Constitution. He argued that the Constitution prohibited states from regulating interstate commerce and that the Mississippi prohibition was just such a regulation.

Groves came to the Court against the backdrop of the 1837 decision in *New York v. Miln*. In *Miln*, the Court had been faced with an analogous challenge to a New York statute that required the masters of vessels to make detailed reports on passengers brought into the port of New York from other states or countries, to post a bond for each such person brought into the port, and to remove any whom the mayor of New York determined likely to become financially dependent on the city government. With only one dissent, the Supreme Court had rejected the challenge, declaring that because the statute dealt only with the movement of people rather than the movement of goods, the law was "a regulation not of commerce but of police." If slaves were to be conceptualized as people rather than property under the Constitution, the same principle would have been decisive in *Groves*.

For obvious reasons, the question of the proper characterization of slaves for constitutional purposes had potentially divisive implications. At the same time, both sides in the dispute over slavery had reason to hope for the rejection of the constitutional challenge in *Groves*. Among the defenders of slavery, even the most ardent proponents of federal power often believed that the slave states should be given a free hand in dealing with the interstate slave trade. Conversely, antislavery forces were no doubt pleased by the substance of the Mississippi restriction on the slave trade and would thus have been disappointed if the restriction had been found unconstitutional.

Against this background, it should not be surprising that a majority of the justices initially sought to avoid the delicate issues raised in *Groves* by holding that the state constitutional provision did not void the note that was before the Court. Over the dissents of Justices Joseph Story of Massachusetts and John McKinley of Alabama, Justice Smith Thompson's majority opinion argued that the Mississippi constitutional provision was not self-executing and observed that implementing legislation had not been passed by the state legislature until 1837, *after* the consummation of the transaction that underlay the promissory note in issue. Thus, Thompson concluded that the holder of the note could collect because state law did not render the note unenforceable, and that it was therefore unnecessary to reach the claim that the state constitutional provision was inconsistent with the federal Constitution.

Justice John McLean, however, refused to be deterred from exploring the potentially explosive issues implicated by *Groves*. McLean conceded that discussion of the federal Constitution was unnecessary to a decision in the case. Nonetheless, he explicitly concluded that federal power to regulate interstate commerce was exclusive, but that because slaves were to be considered "persons" for constitutional purposes, the states had exclusive authority to regulate the interstate slave trade. Although the other justices were clearly annoyed that McLean had foiled their effort to resolve *Groves* without doing anything that might exacerbate sectional tensions, they felt compelled to address the issues that McLean had raised. However, with the exception of a detailed opinion by Justice Henry Baldwin of Pennsylvania, who took sharp issue with McLean's conclusions, the response to McLean's opinion was muted. Chief Justice Roger Brooke Taney wrote a short, bland opinion declining to discuss the scope of federal power over commerce generally but agreeing that Congress had no authority to regulate the interstate slave trade. The remaining justices contented themselves with a statement that in their view, the Mississippi constitutional provision did not run afoul of any federal constitutional prohibition.

Groves was followed quickly by the decision in *United States v. The Amistad*. In *The Amistad*, the Court was faced with a delicate problem arising from the international slave trade. Aversion to that trade crossed sectional lines. Even as early as the late eighteenth century, many of those who supported slavery or viewed it as a necessary evil often condemned the practice of transporting hitherto free Africans to the United States to be sold into bondage. Indeed, in an early draft of the Declaration of Independence, Thomas Jefferson condemned King George for "wag[ing] a cruel war against human nature itself, violating its most sacred right of life and liberty in the persons of a distant people who have never offended him, captivating them and carrying them into slavery in another hemisphere, or to incur miserable death in their transportation thither." However, in the face of Southern opposition, this language was dropped from the final version of the Declaration.

At the Constitutional Convention, the dispute over the issue culminated with the adoption of Article I, Section 9, paragraph 1, which prohibited congressional interference with the international slave trade until the year 1808. The legislative history of this clause is relatively straightforward. The original report of the convention's Committee on Detail contained a provision forbidding federal regulation of the slave trade as well as a stipulation that navigation acts could be adopted by Congress only with a two-thirds majority. On August 22 a number of delegates, led by George Mason of Virginia, launched a fierce attack on the slave trade clause, while Charles C. Pinckney and John Rutledge of South Carolina declared that the prohibition on federal regulation was a sine qua non for the participation of the Deep South states in the Union. Pinckney and Rutledge were supported by Roger Sherman and Oliver Ellsworth of Connecticut. Gouverneur Morris suggested that the slave trade issue could be dealt with as part of a compromise package that included other commerce-related measures. The issue was then recommitted to committee, and a bargain was struck. The delegates from the Deep South states — who generally opposed federal power to adopt navigation acts — agreed to allow the passage of navigation acts by a simple majority, and in return the delegates from Massachusetts and New Hampshire agreed to support a temporary ban on federal prohibition of the slave trade. The agreement was consummated on August 23. Over the objections of Virginia, New Jersey, Pennsylvania, and Delaware, the convention adopted the current provision, which protected the right of states to allow the importation of slaves until 1808.

Immediately after the constitutional bar expired, Congress acted to prohibit the international slave trade. The terms of the statutory prohibition were strengthened in 1819. But the importation of substantial numbers of slaves from Africa continued even after the adoption of the federal statutes. Smuggling human cargo was highly profitable, and enforcement of the legal sanctions was at times lax. In order to circumvent American law, smugglers often sailed under the flags of nations that continued to allow the slave trade. Seizures of such vessels gave rise to a variety of disputes that found their way to the federal courts.

Prior to 1841, the Supreme Court's most important pronouncements on the slave trade had come in its 1825 decision in *The Antelope*. There the Court had been called upon to adjudicate the status of over 250 Africans found on board the *Antelope*, a Spanish vessel that had been engaged in the slave trade off the coast of Africa when it, along with three Portuguese vessels and an American ship similarly engaged, had been captured by the *Columbia*, a privateer flying the flag of a short-lived Latin American revolutionary state. Under the control of a prize crew, the *Antelope*, with many African prisoners on board, sailed in tandem with the *Columbia* until the latter was wrecked off the coast of Brazil. At that time a number of Africans who were on board the *Columbia* were transferred to the *Antelope*, which was subsequently intercepted by an American revenue cutter off the coast of the United States and brought to the port of Savannah. The captain of the *Columbia* and the master of the revenue cutter both claimed property rights in the Africans; in addition, officials of the Spanish government and the Portuguese government intervened, each asserting the rights of their own nationals. William Wirt, representing the interests of the Africans, argued that the Africans should be deemed free people. He contended that the Supreme Court should hold that the slave trade was unlawful under international law and that, therefore, the American courts should consider the trade unlawful even when conducted by foreign ships.

Although ruling in favor of the Africans on a number of other points, the Supreme Court rejected this assertion. Speaking for the Court, Chief Justice John Marshall conceded that the slave trade was "contrary to the law of nature" but also noted that the trade was legal under "the usages [and] national acts" of the portions of the world in which the *Columbia* and *Antelope* had acquired their cargo. Thus, emphasizing that he was acting as a "jurist" rather than a "moralist," Marshall concluded that he was compelled to hold that the slave trade did not violate the law of nations.

The facts of *The Amistad* were much more dramatic than those that had given rise to *The Antelope*. In *The Amistad*, a group of captured Africans was taken to Cuba by Spanish slave traders. Under both Spanish law and a treaty with England, Spaniards were forbidden to engage in the slave trade. Nonetheless, when the *Amistad* landed in Cuba, the Cuban authorities provided documents certifying that the Africans were in fact the legal property of the slave traders. While being transported from Havana to another Cuban port, the Africans revolted, killing the captain of the *Amistad* and taking control of the ship. They ordered the purported owner of the vessel and another of the remaining Spaniards to sail the ship back to Africa. However, for a month the Spaniards deceived the Africans, sailing the *Amistad* on a course that eventually brought it off the coast of Long Island. There, after some of the Africans had gone ashore to obtain supplies, the ship was taken into custody by an officer of a U.S. naval vessel. The Africans were then incarcerated pending resolution of charges of murder and conflicting civil claims regarding their status.

The murder charges were dismissed relatively early in the proceedings. Nonetheless, speaking on behalf of the owners of the vessel, the Spanish government asserted that the government of the United

States was bound to surrender both the ship and the Africans to Spanish custody. The Spanish based their claim on Pinckney's Treaty of 1795, which provided for the restoration of "all ships and merchandise, . . . which shall be rescued out of the hands of any pirates or robbers on the high seas." Conversely, the Africans wished to be declared free men.

Both sides had important American allies in the political and legal struggle that followed. Abolitionists in Connecticut formed a committee that provided for the legal defense of the Africans in the criminal proceedings as well as the civil actions. By contrast, Southerners generally supported the Spanish claimants. Responding to an early victory by the Africans in federal court, one Southern commentator described the result as "a base outrage . . . on all the sympathies of civilized life." The Spanish also had the backing of the administration of the administration of President Martin Van Buren. At the urging of Secretary of State John Forsythe of Georgia, Attorney General Felix Grundy of Tennessee issued an official opinion that supported the Spanish claim, and, in anticipation of a Spanish victory in the courts, at one point an American naval vessel was made available to transport the Africans to Spain.

The Supreme Court disagreed with the Van Buren administration. With only Justice Baldwin dissenting, the Court found against the Spanish claimants. Speaking for the majority, Justice Story argued that the evidence clearly established that the claimants had violated Spanish law by capturing the Africans. Therefore, the Africans could not be considered "pirates or robbers" within the meaning of the treaty, notwithstanding "the dreadful acts, by which they asserted their liberty and took possession of the *Amistad*." Story rejected the claim that the Court was required to honor the Spanish documents that purported to establish the rights of the Spanish claimants. He also dismissed the contention that the treaty forbade an inquiry into the bona fides of the documents and asserted that "although public documents of the government, accompanying property found on board of the private ships of a foreign nation, certainly are to be deemed prima facie evidence of the facts which they purport to state, yet they are always open to be impugned for fraud; and whether that fraud be in the original obtaining of these documents, or in the subsequent fraudulent and illegal use of them, when it is satisfactorily established, it overthrows all their sanctity, and destroys them as proof."

Story also emphasized the magnitude of the interest of the Africans in *The Amistad:*

> It is also a most important consideration in the present case, which ought not to be lost sight of, that, supposing these African negroes not to be slaves, but kidnapped, and free negroes, the treaty with Spain cannot be obligatory upon them, and the United States are bound to respect their rights as much as those of the Spanish subjects. . . . If the contest were about any goods on board this ship, to which American citizens asserted a title, which was denied by the Spanish claimants, there could be no doubt of the right of such American citizens to litigate their claims before any competent American tribunal, notwithstanding the treaty with Spain. A fortiori, the doctrine must apply where human life and human liberty are in issue. . . . The treaty with Spain never could have intended to take away the equal rights of all Foreigners, who should contest their claims before any of our Courts, to equal justice; or to deprive such foreigners of the protection given them by other treaties, or by the general law of nations.

Against this background, Story had no difficulty in concluding that the Africans should not be returned to the custody of their former captors.

The Amistad was a clear victory for the opponents of slavery. Moreover, the decision of the Southern justices to join in the opinion of the Court demonstrated their willingness to vote against the proslavery political forces in some circumstances. By contrast, the actions of the Court as a whole and the Southern justices in particular were far more ambiguous in *Prigg v. Pennsylvania.*

Prigg forced the Court to squarely confront the obligations of the Northerners and their state governments to aid slaveowners who claimed rights under the fugitive slave clause of the Constitution. In marked contrast to the intense struggles over the slave trade and the treatment of slaves in the basis of representation, the inclusion of the fugitive slave clause had generated little controversy. The provision clearly provided slaveowners with rights beyond those they had enjoyed under the Articles of Confederation, but even antislavery forces apparently conceded that, so long as slavery was legal in any state, slaveowners should be entitled to the protections established by the clause. Thus, there was no objection to the basic principle of Article IV, Section 2, paragraph 2 when it was proposed at the Constitutional Convention. Although Charles Pinckney of South Carolina emphasized the benefit that the fugitive slave clause provided to slaveowners in his defense of the Constitution, antislavery forces rarely cited the issue of fugitive slaves as a reason to oppose ratification.

While clearly establishing the proposition that free states could not emancipate fugitives by operation of law, the fugitive slave clause left a number of critical questions unanswered. One of the most important of these questions was whether Congress possessed constitutional authority to enact enforcement legislation. Unlike the full faith and credit clause — also included in Article IV — the fugitive slave clause does not explicitly grant Congress such authority, instead providing only that the fugitive "shall be delivered up on Claim of the Party to whom . . . Service or Labour may be due." Moreover, no power to enforce the fugitive slave clause was included in Article I, section 8, where the powers of Congress generally were listed.

Nonetheless, soon after the ratification of the Constitution, Congress enacted a federal statute establishing procedures for the recovery of escaped slaves. The chain of events leading to congressional action began with a dispute between Virginia and Pennsylvania over a request by the Pennsylvania authorities for the extradition of three citizens of Virginia. The Virginians had been indicted for allegedly violating the Pennsylvania Antikidnapping Act of 1788 by removing an African American from Pennsylvania to Virginia, where he was enslaved. Article IV, Section 2, paragraph 2 of the Constitution — the extradition clause, a companion to the fugitive slave clause — seemed to require the state of Virginia to "deliver up" the indicted Virginians to Pennsylvania. However, the case was politically sensitive, and the states reached an impasse after the attorney general of Virginia took the view that the Virginia authorities were not required to honor the extradition request in the absence of federal legislation prescribing the procedures to be followed. Notwithstanding the lack of explicit constitutional authority to adopt enforcement legislation, Congress moved quickly to establish extradition procedures. The Fugitive Slave Act of 1793 was adopted as an adjunct to the extradition bill.

The new federal statute allowed a slaveowner or his agent to seize an alleged fugitive and bring him or her before either a federal judge or a local magistrate. Upon "proof [of ownership] to the satisfaction" of that official, which could be provided either by affidavit or oral testimony, a certificate would be issued that allowed the removal of the alleged slave to the state from which he or she was purported to have fled. The statute also provided that anyone who knowingly and willingly obstructed a claimant in his effort to recover a slave would be subject to a $500 penalty, payable to the claimant.

The statute left a number of issues in doubt. For example, it was unclear whether the owner retained the common-law right of "recaption" — the right to reclaim an escaped slave by self-help and to return him to service without the benefit of government intervention or sanction. Moreover, the statute did not address the constitutional status of state laws that either established protection against kidnapping for free African Americans or provided slaveowners with additional remedies. Finally, the constitutionality of parts of the federal law remained in doubt for much of the early nineteenth century, as antislavery theorists not only claimed that alleged fugitives were constitutionally entitled to jury trials but also at times denied that Congress possessed any authority to enforce the fugitive slave clause.

All of these issues were hotly debated against the context of ongoing and escalating friction between the slave states and the free states over the issue of fugitive slaves. The slave states pressed for measures that would both simplify the task of slaveowners seeking to recover fugitives and provide maximum governmental support for the enterprise. The governments of the free states, by contrast, faced a more complex dilemma in their efforts to craft appropriate policies. On one hand, Northern states sought to protect genuinely free African Americans from being sent into slavery in the South as "fugitives"; on the other, the free states were often cognizant of their obligations to their Southern brethren and sought to preserve sectional harmony. As antislavery sentiment grew in the North during the nineteenth century, the provisions of state "personal liberty" laws imposed increasing restrictions on the ability to recapture fugitives. Not surprisingly, tensions mounted between North and South.

The evolution of the state laws of Pennsylvania was fairly typical. In 1780 the state legislature passed a law providing for the gradual abolition of slavery within the state. Because emancipation was not immediate, slaveowners were able to devise a variety of strategies designed to avoid the operation of the state law. Some of these strategies involved the transportation of young African Americans or pregnant slaves south-ward to states that remained committed to the institution of slavery. To combat this problem, in 1788 Pennsylvania adopted its first antikidnapping statute. This statute prohibited slaves from being removed from the state without their consent, as well as the consent of parents in the case of their children. The statute also specifically outlawed the practice of kidnapping free African Americans with the intent to sell them into slavery, providing that violators would be subject to a jail sentence and a fine of 100 pounds.

In 1820, with sectional tensions rising over the issue of slavery in Missouri and a number of prominent citizens expressing displeasure with the provision for summary proceedings in the Fugitive Slave Act, the Pennsylvania state legislature passed a stronger personal-liberty law. The new statute stiffened the penalties for the kidnapping of free African Americans. More importantly, it prohibited local aldermen and justices of the peace from taking jurisdiction over cases involving runaways. Thus, the 1820 statute made it substantially more difficult for claimants to locate an official who could act to enforce their rights under the federal Fugitive Slave Act of 1793.

Officials in the neighboring slave state of Maryland were seriously disturbed by the 1820 statute. They sent commissioners to the Pennsylvania state legislature, carrying with them proposed revisions that were far more favorable to those seeking to recover alleged fugitives. An intense political struggle ensued, and in 1826 a revised state law dealing with fugitive slaves was adopted by the legislature. The new law was clearly a compromise between the demands of Maryland slaveholders and those of the antislavery forces in Pennsylvania. While abolishing the common-law right of recaption in Pennsylvania, the new law also reinstated the jurisdiction of local judicial officials over actions to recover fugitives. At the same time, the procedural requirements for the issuance of a certificate of removal were much more stringent than the federal law. The alleged runaway could not be detained without an affidavit from the claimant providing a detailed description of the basis for his claim. Moreover, the oath of the owner or other interested persons would not suffice to support a certificate of removal, and the alleged slave was entitled to introduce evidence to refute the slaveowner's claim.

Although one of the Maryland commissioners described the Pennsylvania law as "eminently useful . . . because it is a pledge that the states will adhere to the original obligations of the confederacy," the representatives of the state of Maryland were far from entirely satisfied with the substance of the new Pennsylvania statute. Thus, it should not be surprising that the issue of fugitive slaves continued to be a source of tension between the two states. The facts of *Prigg* reflected this tension.

The case arose from the claim of Margaret Ashmore that Margaret Morgan was a slave who in 1832 had fled from Ashmore's home in northern Maryland to southern Pennsylvania. Four Marylanders, including Edward Prigg, pursued Morgan five years later and, following the procedures outlined in the Pennsylvania statute, obtained a warrant from a justice of the peace directing that she be taken into custody. However, the justice of the peace eventually refused to issue a certificate of removal. Nonetheless, the Marylanders removed Morgan to Maryland, where, after a hearing, a county court determined that Morgan was indeed a slave owned by Ashmore.

At this stage a Pennsylvania court indicted Prigg and his companions for violating the 1826 statute. The governor of Pennsylvania demanded that they be extradited. A period of intense negotiations followed, as the governor of Maryland and the state legislature of Maryland sought to persuade Pennsylvania officials to have the indictments dismissed. When this effort failed, the Pennsylvania legislature adopted a statute that allowed Prigg to be tried in a manner that would ensure that the issues raised by the case could ultimately be resolved by the Supreme Court.

Prigg required the justices to grapple with a variety of related but analytically separable types of issues. The case clearly presented a conflict between two competing claims of right. Not surprisingly, Southerners tended to emphasize the right of slaveholders to recover their property. Antislavery theorists, on the other hand, focused strongly on the right of free blacks to have the protections necessary to avoid being erroneously sent into slavery. *Prigg* also raised questions of federalism — the proper allocation of authority between the federal and state governments in cases involving fugitive slaves. All of the justices were obviously aware of the sectional tensions surrounding the issue of fugitive slaves and the fact that their decision could either exacerbate or reduce those tensions.

Joseph Story spoke for the majority. Story was a committed opponent of slavery; at the same time, he hated abolitionists and was acutely cognizant of the need to preserve sectional harmony. His opinion in *Prigg* reflected all of these influences. The opinion began promisingly for the antislavery forces, adopting the position of *Somerset v. Stewart*, the legal mainstay of the antislavery movement, and declaring that "by the general law of nations, no nation is bound to recognize the state of slavery, as to foreign slaves found within its territorial dominions, when it is in opposition to its own policy and institutions, in favor of other nations where slavery is recognized [because] slavery is deemed to be a mere municipal regulation, founded upon and limited to the range of the territorial laws." Despite this ringing antislavery rhetoric, Story then proceeded to outline and defend a set of conclusions that were in many cases more favorable to the proslavery position.

Story began by arguing that the fugitive slave clause was central to the creation and maintenance of the Union, asserting that the clause was "of the last importance to the safety and security of the southern states and could not have been surrendered by them, without endangering their whole property in slaves." He further contended that in the absence of some constitutional provision, the issue of fugitive slaves "would have created the most bitter animosities, and engendered perpetual strife between the different states." He then described the scope of the fugitive slave clause in sweeping terms, asserting that "any state law or . . . regulation, which interrupts, limits, delays or postpones the right of the owner to the immediate possession of the slave, and the immediate command of his service and labor, operates, *pro tanto* a discharge of the slave therefrom. . . . The question is not one of quantity or degree, but of withholding or controlling the incidents of a positive and absolute right."

Story's treatment of the right of recaption followed logically from this characterization. He noted that, under the principles of the common law, the right of ownership in property carried with it the right to recover the property by self-help. He further observed that, by its terms, the fugitive slave clause required even nonslave states to recognize the owner's property right in the escaped slave. Thus, Story proclaimed that he had "not the slightest hesitation in holding, that . . . the owner of a slave is clothed with entire authority, in every state in the

Union, to seize and recapture his slave, whenever he can do it, without any breach of the peace or any illegal violence."

Having embraced the proslavery position on recaption, Story next addressed the respective roles of the state and federal governments in enforcing the fugitive slave clause. Story began this portion of the opinion by observing that government aid would often be necessary for the claimant to recover the fugitive, and that the clause itself, which provided that the slave "shall be delivered up, on claim of the [putative master]," seemed to contemplate government enforcement. Against the background of this premise, he turned to the question of *which* government was charged with the duty of enforcement.

On this point, Story relied on the general principle that "where the end is required, the means are given; and where the duty is enjoined, the ability to perform it is contemplated to exist, on the part of the functionaries to whom it is entrusted." Thus, Story argued that because the fugitive slave clause was found in the federal Constitution, "the natural inference certainly is, that the national government is clothed with the appropriate authority and functions to enforce it." He scoffed at the notion that the lack of a specific enforcement provision was fatal to this contention, declaring that "if this be the true interpretation of the constitution, it must, in a great measure, fail to attain many of its avowed objects, as a security of rights and recognition of duties," and noting that "[Congress] has, on various occasions, exercised powers that were necessary and proper as means to carry into effect rights expressly given, and duties expressly enjoined thereby." Thus, after reviewing in detail the specific provisions of the Fugitive Slave Act of 1793, he concluded that, with one specific exception, the act was "clearly constitutional, in all its leading provisions." Story thereby implicitly rejected the claim that a jury trial was required before an alleged fugitive could be seized and delivered to a claimant.

While emphasizing the power of Congress to enforce the fugitive slave clause, Story downplayed the role that state governments were to play in vindicating the claims of putative owners. First, noting that "the clause is found in the national constitution, and not in that of any state [and] does not point out any state functionaries, or any state action, to carry its provisions into effect," Story argued that the Fugitive Slave Act was unconstitutional insofar as it *required* state officials to participate in the recovery of fugitives. Moreover, Story concluded that the power to enforce the clause was vested *exclusively* in the federal government, contending that "the nature of the provision and the objects to be attained by it require that it should be controlled by one and the same will and act uniformly by the same system of regulations throughout the Union." Otherwise, he argued, the right established by the Constitution "would never, in a practical sense, be the same in all the States [but] might be enforced in some States, retarded or limited in others and denied as compulsory in many, if not in all." Thus, in Story's view, states could not pass statutes designed to vindicate the claims of owners even if the operation of those statutes did not in any way conflict with the procedures mandated by the federal statute.

These elements of Story's opinion in *Prigg* rested almost entirely on the doctrine of federal supremacy. He did make two concessions to the principle of state autonomy, however. First, as already noted, he concluded that state officers could not be compelled to enforce the federal statute, although they were free to do so if required by state law. Second, he distinguished sharply between regulation of the owner's right to retake fugitive slaves and the police power of the state, holding that, under the latter rubric, states retained "full jurisdiction to arrest and restrain runaway slaves, and remove them from their borders and otherwise secure themselves against their depredations and evil example."

Justice Story's opinion seems to have garnered the support of a majority of justices on all points. However, Story was joined in full by only three justices — John Catron of Tennessee, John McKinley of Alabama, and James Moore Wayne of Georgia. Some modern commentators would no doubt characterize this support as evidence of a pro-Southern orientation in Story's analysis. R. Kent Newmyer, for example, concludes that "*Prigg* went to the South, or so at least a plain reading of [Justice Story's] opinion would indicate," and Don E. Fehrenbacher describes Story's opinion as "emphatically proslavery in tone and substance." Those who take this view can cite some evidence from contemporary reactions to the decision. Although *Prigg* does not seem to have generated great excitement in the mainstream Northern press, abolitionists roundly condemned the decision, whereas (apparently without having had access to the text of Story's opinion) the *Baltimore Sun* declared that *Prigg* was "all that Maryland can desire, and will be particularly agreeable to the slaveholders of the South."

Nonetheless, Catron, McKinley, and Wayne almost certainly *believed* that they were making significant concessions to the North in endorsing the ban on supplemental state remedies for slaveowners pursuing fugitives and by the declaration that state officials could not be forced to cooperate in the enforcement of the federal statute. In the antebellum world, where state government officials vastly outnumbered representatives of the federal government, these limitations were of great practical significance to slaveholders. Indeed, from an early date Southerners had pressed for greater state participation in the rendition of fugitive slaves and in 1817 nearly succeeded in having such a requirement enacted into federal law. In *Prigg* itself, two other Southern justices — Roger Brooke Taney of Maryland and Peter V. Daniel of Virginia — argued vigorously that effective enforcement of the fugitive slave clause required participation by state officials. Conversely, while conceding that the ban on state enforcement measures might well hinder the efforts of slaveowners to recapture fugitives, Wayne asserted that Southerners should be willing to pay that price in order to "remove . . . those causes which have contributed more than any other to disturb that harmony which is essential to the continuance of the Union." Against this background, the concurrence of the three Southern justices in *Prigg* is most plausibly viewed as a reflection of a decision to sacrifice some of the interests of slaveowners in the hope of minimizing the sectional friction created by the dispute over fugitive slaves.

In short, in *Prigg* both the antislavery Story and a majority of the Southern justices showed a willingness to make concessions in order to promote sectional harmony. In this respect, however one evaluates the merits of the Court's analysis of the fugitive slave clause, the case fits comfortably with the pattern of the contemporaneous decisions in *Groves v. Slaughter* and *The Amistad. Dred Scott*, by contrast, reflects a quite different dynamic, one in which the Southern justices in particular demonstrated an unyielding militancy in defense of slavery. This change in perspective was a by-product of the political struggles of the 1840s and 1850s.

CHAPTER 4

Slavery in the Territories, 1842–1856

The admission of Missouri in 1821 did not entirely still the controversy over the expansion of slavery. While Southerners typically did not challenge the principles established in the Missouri Compromise, some Northerners continued to voice opposition to the recognition of slavery even in those areas south of the Missouri Compromise line. As early as 1836, the dispute bubbled to the surface during the debate in the House of Representatives over the admission of Arkansas. The proposed state constitution prohibited the legislature from emancipating slaves without the consent of their masters. Rep. John Quincy Adams moved to amend the bill admitting Arkansas to provide that "nothing in this Act shall be construed by Congress to the article in the constitution in relation to slavery or the emancipation of slaves." Rep. Henry A. Wise of Virginia complained that the introduction of this amendment essentially revived the issues that had purportedly been resolved by the Missouri Compromise. This characterization of the Adams proposal was disputed by Rep. George N. Briggs of Massachusetts, who observed that adoption of the proposal would neither delay the admission of Arkansas nor force changes in the proposed state constitution. At the same time, Briggs averred that "upon this subject of slavery I cannot go the breadth of a hair beyond the obligations imposed on me by [the Constitution]. I never can consent . . . to give a vote [to] sanction the principle, or extend the existence of human slavery." Rep. Gideon Hard of New York took a more extreme view, arguing that any state constitution that recognized the legality of slavery was inconsistent with the federal Constitution's guarantee of a republican form of government. Although no formal vote was ever taken on the Adams amendment, fifty Northern congressmen ultimately opposed the unamended bill for the admission of Arkansas. Florida was admitted as a slave state in 1845 only over similar objections. Nonetheless, the dispute over the expansion of slavery did not reemerge as a major national issue until the United States acquired vast new territories in the 1840s. The spark that reignited the conflict was the struggle over the annexation of Texas.

The sequence of events that led to the acquisition of Texas can be traced to the Adams-Onis Treaty of 1819, in which the United States renounced its claims to Texas in return for the agreement of the Spanish government to sell Florida to the United States. Subsequently, efforts were made to purchase Texas by the administrations of both John Quincy Adams and Andrew Jackson. The Mexican government rebuffed these overtures. The situation became more complex after Texas declared its independence from Mexico in 1836. The victories of the Texans on the battlefield, together with the request of their fledgling government for annexation in November 1836, set off an intense debate in the United States over the appropriate course of action for the American government.

The debate over Texas took on a strong sectional tone. Many Southerners favored annexation, whereas Northern opinion was generally hostile. Northern opponents included not only antislavery Whigs but also Van Buren Democrats, who (though often derided for deferring unduly to their Southern counterparts) worried that a serious effort to annex Texas would disrupt the sectional harmony that they strove mightily to preserve. Against this background, a petition circulated widely by the American Anti-Slavery Society complained that "six or eight" slave states might ultimately be carved out of Texas, leaving the South in complete control of the national government. In addition, the governments of eight Northern states formally protested against annexation. Conversely, on January 4, 1838, Sen. William C. Campbell of South Carolina offered a resolution urging the annexation of Texas whenever it could be done "consistently with the public faith and treaty stipulations of the United States" and without disrupting relations with Mexico. On June 14, seven senators from the slave states joined with their united Northern colleagues to table the resolution by a vote of 24-14.

With neither party's leadership having any apparent inclination to press the issue, the prospects for annexation seemed dim. However, the situation changed dramatically in 1841, when John Tyler of Virginia succeeded to the presidency after the death of William Henry Harrison.

Tyler — an apostate Whig — pursued the annexation of Texas with an enthusiasm that stemmed in part from a sincere commitment to the principle of national expansion and in part from a desire to use the issue to create an independent power base for his administration. His representatives successfully negotiated a treaty of annexation, and the treaty was submitted to the Senate for ratification on April 22, 1844.

Issues of slavery and sectional relations played a major role in the dispute that followed. The visibility of these issues was heightened by a letter written by Secretary of State John C. Calhoun to Richard Pakenham, the English minister to the United States. The Pakenham letter was a response to a dispatch from Lord Aberdeen, the English foreign secretary, in which Aberdeen acknowledged that England had been urging the government of Texas to abolish slavery but also averred that the English would not seek to "compel" that course of action or "unduly control" the actions of Texas in this regard. Calhoun — the leading apostle of Southern sectionalism — answered by *explicitly* defending the treaty between the United States and Texas on the ground that annexation was necessary to protect the South from the abolitionist designs of the English.

Calhoun's motives for making this intemperate assertion have been extensively debated by historians. Nonetheless, when the Pakenham letter was released to the Senate, its impact was immediate and predictable. Calhoun's missive provided impetus to the claim that annexation was simply a device to enhance the position of the slave power in the federal government.

Against this background, the treaty was overwhelmingly rejected in the Senate by a vote of 35-16. Despite the importance of the slavery issue, the pattern of the votes clearly indicates that other considerations were significant as well. With the sole exception of Sen. John Henderson of Mississippi, both Northern and Southern Whigs voted solidly against the treaty. Conversely, all slave-state Democrats except Sen. Thomas Hart Benton of Missouri voted for the treaty. Only free-state Democrats were split, with five out of twelve voting in favor of ratification.

The defeat of the treaty did not signal the end of the controversy over the annexation of Texas. In large measure because of Martin Van Buren's opposition to the annexation of Texas, the Democratic Convention in its quest for a presidential nominee passed over Van Buren —

a New Yorker who was the leader of the Northern Democrats — in favor of James K. Polk, the obscure proannexation former governor of Tennessee. The convention also adopted a platform that strongly favored the acquisition of Texas. As expected, the Whigs nominated Henry Clay to succeed Tyler. The Whig platform opposed annexation. The electorate was thus presented with a clear choice on the issue of annexation.

Polk won a narrow victory, with a plurality in the popular vote of less than 40,000 out of more than 2.7 million votes cast and a vote of 170-105 in the electoral college. Polk's election substantially changed the political dynamic of the annexation issue. Annexationists claimed a popular mandate for their position and pressed their cause with renewed enthusiasm. However, although the strength of the Whigs in the Senate had been substantially reduced by the election, even in the new Congress Democrats were well short of the two-thirds majority necessary to ratify a treaty. Thus, the only viable option was to proceed by admitting Texas as a state through a joint resolution of Congress — an idea that Tyler had entertained even before the defeat of the treaty.

Issues of constitutionality aside, the use of this device brought the question of slavery even more clearly to the fore. Although under most proposals the entire area of Texas was to be initially admitted as a single slave state, no one at the time took the view that the new state would remain undivided. Both supporters and opponents believed that, as its population grew and dispersed more widely, Texas would eventually be divided into a number of smaller states. Much of the debate over the various forms of the joint resolution focused on the impact that the admission of Texas would have on the balance of power between North and South. For example, Whig Rep. Robert C. Winthrop of Massachusetts complained bitterly that a measure that allowed several slave states to be carved from Texas would upset the "equipoise" between the free states and the slave states, giving the South a "preponderance." Similarly, Whig Rep. Joshua Giddings of Ohio asserted that the ultimate settlement "has given the southern portion the balance of power, and has subjected the free labor of the North . . . to the tender mercies of a slave-holding oligarchy." North-erners pressed for assurances that slavery would be outlawed in at least some of the states that would ultimately be carved out of Texas.

By contrast, Southerners such as Democratic Rep. Howell Cobb of Georgia contended that Northerners such as Winthrop and Giddings took the acquisition of Texas out of context. Cobb observed that a vast area north of the Missouri Compromise line in both the former Louisiana Purchase and the Oregon Territory was steadily being organized and settled and promised to yield a substantial number of nonslave states in the future. By contrast, he noted that, except for Florida, which was to be admitted as a state in 1845, the United States claimed almost no territory south of 36 degrees, 30 minutes. Cobb argued that even the annexation of Texas and the possibility of eventually dividing the state into four slave states would not come near to balancing the advantage of the North in this regard. Thus, although many Southerners saw Texas "as a counterpoise to the growing and preponderant strength of the North," many also agreed with Democratic Rep. Robert B. Rhett of South Carolina, who contended that "the South was in a minority, and was destined ever to be so."

Against this background, the House of Representatives ultimately adopted the proposal of Rep. Milton Brown, a Tennessee Whig, which basically incorporated the principles of the Missouri Compromise. Opponents of slavery rejected the Brown proposal as inadequate, noting that the part of Texas north of the line was minuscule at best. Thus, twenty-eight Northern Democrats voted against the proposal. In addition, House Whigs generally remained adamant in their opposition to any scheme for annexation, with only seven Southern Whigs supporting Brown. Nonetheless, his proposal gained a 120-98 majority.

Supporters of annexation faced a more difficult task in the Senate. There, the Whigs continued to hold a slender majority in the lame-duck session, so annexationists could not prevail without some Whig defections. Moreover, supporters of annexation would need the support of the seven Van Buren Democrats who had opposed the annexation treaty. The leader of the Van Burenites in the Senate was Sen. Thomas Hart Benton of Missouri — the only slave-state Democrat who had voted against the treaty. Early in the session, Benton put forth a resolution that would have authorized the president to negotiate with the government of Mexico for the acquisition of Texas while at the same time providing that, if acquired, Texas would ultimately be divided equally between free states and slave states. Later, under pressure from both the Missouri state legislature and Andrew

Jackson, Benton introduced a quite different resolution, authorizing the president to negotiate annexation with the government of *Texas*. Southerners were dissatisfied because the new resolution did not resolve the issue of slavery. They suggested to Benton that he include the territorial provisions of the Brown resolution in his proposal. However, Northern Democrats objected to this suggestion. The impasse was resolved by combining the Benton and Brown resolutions, giving the president the option of either offering annexation to Texas under the terms outlined in the House proposal or reopening negotiations. Believing they had assurances that Polk would pursue the Benton option, the Van Burenites threw their support behind the combined proposal. On February 27, 1845, the resolution was adopted by the Senate by a vote of 27-25, with three Southern Whigs joining the united Democrats to provide the margin of victory. The following day the revised proposal passed the House 132-76 on an almost straight party-line vote.

The belief that Polk would renegotiate the conditions of annexation was critical to Democratic unanimity and thus to the success of the resolution in the Senate. In essence, this belief allowed the Van Buren Democrats to satisfy the demands of loyalty to the party platform without committing themselves to acquiescence in annexation under terms they believed unacceptable. In particular, it left open the option of refighting the battle over the division of Texas into free and slave states when the renegotiated terms were once again presented to Congress. Indeed, it was quite possible that renegotiation would doom the entire project. Calhoun, for example, feared that pursuit of the Benton alternative would ultimately result in the submission of a new treaty, which would likely die in the Senate because of Whig opposition.

However, subsequent events did not follow the course envisioned by the Van Burenites. They were stunned when the lame-duck Tyler presented the government of Texas with the terms of the Brown resolution. Polk chose not to disavow Tyler's actions, and Texas accepted Tyler's offer. Thus, Texas was admitted to the Union with the division between potential free and slave states established by the terms of the Brown formulation.

Without question, Northerners were generally dissatisfied with the resolution of the status of slavery in Texas. Nonetheless, in a very real sense, the final settlement did nothing more than reaffirm the basic approach of the Missouri Compromise. Like the Missouri Compromise itself, the terms under which Texas was admitted resolved all outstanding controversial issues related to the expansion of slavery. Thus, while leaving some residual bitterness, the circumstances surrounding the annexation of Texas would no doubt have soon faded into the background of American politics if no other events had influenced the situation.

The difficulty was that the acquisition of Texas led directly to war with Mexico. The war began on April 25, 1846, with an armed clash between American and Mexican forces in an area of southern Texas claimed by both nations. Polk saw the war as an opportunity to acquire additional territory. He coveted much of the northernmost territory then held by Mexico, including what is now the American Southwest as well as "California and the fine bay of San Francisco." Despite the fact that much of the territory sought by Polk and his allies was north of the Missouri Compromise line, Northern Whigs charged that the war was being prosecuted for the purpose of adding slave territory to the United States and thus enhancing the influence of the slave power on the federal government.

By late 1846, Northern Democrats felt they had new reason to distrust their Southern colleagues. Soon thereafter, the dispute over Oregon strained sectional relations still further, particularly within the Democratic party. Prior to 1844, both the United States and Great Britain had asserted claims to the entire Oregon territory — an area that ran from the southern boundary of the modern state of Oregon north to a latitude of 54 degrees, 40 minutes. In 1827 the two nations agreed to jointly occupy the territory until either a final settlement could be reached or the agreement was abrogated by one of the parties. Seeking to gain exclusive control of the harbor at Puget Sound, the United States repeatedly offered to divide the territory at the forty-ninth parallel. The British, by contrast, argued that the boundary should be established by the Columbia River, much of which is below the forty-seventh parallel.

The election of 1844 brought the issue to a head. In an effort to counter the argument that Democratic support for the annexation of Texas was a surrender to the slave power, the Democratic platform for the election called for the United States to demand the entire Oregon territory. In his inaugural address, Polk publicly reiterated his support for the platform position, declaring that "our title to [all of] the country of Oregon is 'clear and unquestionable.'" Taking their lead from Polk, Northern Democrats pressed hard for the abrogation of the joint occupation agreement in both the Senate and the House of Representatives. They were shocked and angered when a treaty resolving the dispute was signed on June 15, 1846. Under the terms of the treaty, the forty-ninth parallel was established as the boundary between the United States and Canada. The sole exception was the southern tip of Vancouver Island, which did not become part of the United States. Further, the right to free navigation of the Columbia River was limited to the ships of the Hudson Bay Company, which had long maintained a number of fur-trading outposts on the river.

The treaty might plausibly have been characterized as a diplomatic victory for the United States, which gained almost everything it had requested in previous negotiations. Indeed, Lord Palmerston, who soon thereafter became Britain's foreign secretary, observed that "it would have been strange if the Americans had not been pleased with an arrangement which gives them everything which they ever really wanted." Nonetheless, Northern Democrats rebelled against the treaty. The depth of their anger was revealed when the Senate voted on the treaty on June 17. While only two slave-state Democrats voted against the treaty, it was opposed by Northern Democrats by a 12-2 vote. The treaty was ratified only because it was supported unanimously by the Senate Whigs.

The bitterness of Northern Democrats was fueled largely by what they saw as the disparate treatment of Texas and Oregon. Northerners pointed out that they had ultimately provided unanimous support for the annexation of Texas (albeit with the understanding that it would be under the terms of the Benton proposal) but that many of their Southern colleagues had refused to reciprocate during the Oregon controversy. Thus, Democratic Sen. Edward Hannegan of Indiana complained during the debates that Texas and Oregon "were nursed and cradled in the same cradle — the [Democratic Convention of 1844]. There was not a moment's hesitation, until Texas was admitted; but the moment she was admitted, the peculiar friends of Texas turned, and were doing all they could to strangle Oregon!" This sense of unfair treatment was magnified by the fact that the Senate was called upon to approve the division of Oregon after war had been declared upon Mexico. Northern Democrats asked why the administration was willing to divide Oregon in order to avoid war with England after refusing to compromise on the Texas boundary in order to avoid war with Mexico.

It was against this background that, representing the interests of a small group of Van Buren Democrats, Democratic Rep. David Wilmot of Pennsylvania introduced his famous proviso during the waning days of the first session of the Twenty-ninth Congress on August 12, 1846. The occasion was a bill that would have appropriated $2 million for the purpose of negotiating a treaty to end the Mexican War and acquiring land from Mexico as an incident to the treaty. Wilmot moved an amendment that would have provided "that, as an express and fundamental condition to the acquisition of any territory from the Republic of Mexico . . . neither slavery nor involuntary servitude shall ever exist in any part of said territory, except for crime, whereof the party shall first be duly convicted."

The Wilmot Proviso was not a product of modern ideas of racial equality. Indeed, in introducing his proposal, Wilmot defended it in starkly racist terms, declaring that "I would preserve for free white labor a fair country, a rich inheritance where the sons of toil, of my own race and color, can live without the disgrace which association with negro slavery brings upon free labor." Nonetheless, many Northerners unquestionably had a strong moral aversion to slavery as an institution, and the proviso embodied this aversion.

The decision to introduce the Wilmot Proviso was also influenced by a number of other factors. In part, the proviso was designed to inoculate Northern supporters of the war against the charge that they supported the expansionist aims of the slave power. In large measure, however, the introduction of the proviso was a response to what many Northern Democrats viewed as unfair treatment by the Polk administration, and their Southern colleagues more generally. Their grievances were not limited to the denial of the nomination to Van Buren and the decision to compromise on the Oregon boundary. Van Burenites generally believed that Polk had unfairly favored their political enemies in the selection of his cabinet. Moreover, Northeasterners were angered by the failure of the recently adopted tariff reforms to incorporate some of their views. Westerners resented Polk's veto of a River and Harbors

Bill that would have benefited their constituents. All of these factors helped create the atmosphere that generated the proviso.

The rules under which the bill was considered allowed almost no debate, but the votes that followed the introduction of Wilmot's amendment provided a clear portent of things to come. In rapid succession, the House rejected an amendment by Democratic Rep. William W. Wick of Indiana that would have applied the Missouri Compromise line to any newly acquired territories, passed the Wilmot amendment, declined to table the bill as amended, and passed the bill. In each case the House was divided almost strictly on sectional lines. With the session coming to a close, maneuvering by both pro- and antiproviso forces led to the death of the bill without action by the Senate.

The issue was revived when Congress reconvened in December. Polk once again sought an appropriation for a treaty with Mexico (this time for $3 million), and on January 4, 1847, Democratic Rep. Preston King of New York moved to attach the Wilmot Proviso to the $3 million bill. The extensive discussions that followed were in many ways reminiscent of the debate over the status of Missouri and Arkansas during the crisis of 1819–1820. To be sure, in one respect the opponents of slavery were in a stronger position in 1847. All parties to the earlier dispute had apparently conceded that in the absence of positive action by Congress, slavery would have been legal in both Missouri and Arkansas. By contrast, slavery was illegal under Mexican law in all of the territory that would have been covered by the Wilmot Proviso. Thus, the supporters of the proviso could legitimately claim that they were simply preventing the introduction of slavery into areas where it had not previously existed.

Southern opposition was based as much on symbolism as on substance. Although some Southerners believed that slavery could flourish in at least part of the territory likely to be acquired from Mexico, others doubted that the land in question (particularly that south of the Missouri Compromise line) was suitable for cultivation by slave labor. However, even those who took the latter position saw the proviso as denying Southerners equal status in the Union. For example, while observing that "I question very much whether slavery, under any circumstances, would ever be transplanted into California. South of 36½ degrees, the territory is comparatively barren, not adapted to slave labor," Democratic Rep. David S. Kaufman of Texas also asserted that "*principle* is dearer to us than *interest*" and the proviso "violates and outrages the principles of the Constitution, and destroys the compromise proposed to the South in 1820." Similarly, Whig Rep. Alexander Stephens of Georgia described the proviso as "an *insult* to the South," an "expression to the world" that Southerners "deserve public censure and national odium."

Such sentiments were exacerbated by the tone of the rhetoric of some who supported the proviso — rhetoric that echoed the acrimonious debate over the admission of Missouri. Thus, for example, Democratic Rep. Bradley R. Wood of New York declared, "This is a national question. . . . It is one in which the North has a deeper and higher stake than the South possibly can have. It is a question whether, in the government of the country, she shall be borne down by your slaveholding, aristocratic institutions that have not in them the first element of Democracy." Describing Virginia as a "worn-out, decaying state" and comparing it unfavorably to Pennsylvania, Whig Rep. James Dixon of Connecticut declared that "slavery is the incubus which has crushed the energies of Virginia, and marred her beauty in the very morning of her youth, with the wan decrepitude of old age." Wilmot himself explicitly compared Michigan to Arkansas, asserting that "within the past twenty years, the former has assumed a high place among the States of this Union. She exhibits at this day all the elements and resources of a great State, cities, flourishing towns and highly cultivated fields, with a population that outnumbers three or four times that of Arkansas. Yet, Arkansas has even a better soil, and superior natural advantages. What is the cause of this disparity? It is slavery . . . and that alone."

Against this background, the proviso issue came to a vote in the House of Representatives on February 15, 1847. After once again defeating efforts to adopt the Missouri Compromise line, the House adopted the antislavery language by a vote of 115-106, with no Northern Whigs and only nineteen Northern Democrats joining the representatives of the slave states in opposition. The amended $3 million bill was then passed and sent to the Senate. There the proviso was defeated by a vote of 31-21, as six Northern Democrats joined the united South in opposition. When the unamended appropriation bill was returned to the House, the Polk administration exerted tremendous political pressure on Northern Democrats. As a result, seven Democrats who had originally supported Wilmot changed their vote, and six more simply absented themselves at the crucial moment. As a result, an effort to reattach the proviso was defeated by a vote of 102-97. The unamended $3 million bill was then passed and sent to the president by a vote of 115-81.

Despite the narrow defeat of the Wilmot Proviso, the sequence of events leading to the ultimate adoption of the $3 million bill increased the unease that many Southerners felt about their position in the Union. Northern states dominated the House of Representatives. The Senate was equally divided, but it appeared likely that nonslave states would soon have a majority in the upper chamber as well. At that point, Calhoun and others feared that "[the South] shall be at the entire mercy of the nonslaveholding states." Further, many Southerners saw the proviso controversy as a demonstration that Northerners were prepared to use their preponderant strength to further cement their dominance and unabashedly advance their own interests at the expense of the South, and that only where diverted by some extrinsic interest — in the case of the proviso, the financing of the Mexican War — would a significant number of Northerners be willing to compromise and take into account what Southerners viewed as their legitimate concerns.

Southerners became even more apprehensive after the struggle over the organization of a government for the newly acquired territory of Oregon. The House of Representatives first considered a bill for the creation of such a government in August 1846, shortly before the Wilmot Proviso was first introduced. On August 6, over the objections of forty-three Southerners, with little discussion, the House adopted a provision outlawing slavery in the new territory. The amended bill then passed on a voice vote, but it was not acted upon by the Senate.

By the time the territorial government bill was reintroduced in the House of Representatives in January 1847, the Wilmot Proviso had dramatically altered the political dynamic. As reported from committee, the Oregon bill effectively barred slavery from Oregon by incorporating the provisions of the Northwest Ordinance by reference. On January 14, Democratic Rep. Armstead Burt of South Carolina introduced a proposal to amend the bill to provide that slavery should be barred "inasmuch as the whole of the said territory lies north of 36 degrees, 30 minutes . . . the line of the Missouri Compromise." Burt's defense of this amendment is notable for its exposition of what was to become the basic Southern position on slavery in the territories — the argument that the Missouri Compromise was unconstitutional, but that the South was nonetheless willing to accept it because it provided a workable basis for sectional coexistence. Northerners, by contrast, refused to accept any implication that slavery should be allowed in territory south of the Missouri Compromise line. On January 15, despite unanimous support from slave-state representatives, the Burt amendment was defeated by a vote of 113-62, with only six free-state representatives registering their support. Over the objection of thirty-five Southern dissenters, the unamended bill passed the next day. Once again, however, the Senate failed to act, largely because of a dispute over whether noncitizens should be allowed to vote in Oregon.

When Congress returned to the consideration of the Oregon question in 1848, its deliberations were complicated by two new factors. The first was the signing of the Treaty of Guadalupe Hidalgo, under which Mexico ceded upper California and New Mexico to the United States. Many senators were less than satisfied with the terms of the treaty. Whigs continued to argue that territorial acquisitions should be limited to northern California, whereas a bisectional group of Democrats pressed for the annexation of the entire nation of Mexico. Nonetheless, the Senate recommended ratification on March 10, and Polk signed the treaty on March 16, thereby giving more concrete form to the issues that had been raised by the Wilmot Proviso.

Efforts to establish a government for Oregon were further complicated by presidential politics. The acrimonious dispute over the Wilmot Proviso had guaranteed that the issue of slavery in the territories would loom large in the election of 1848. Indeed, one Illinois Whig noted that "nothing is talked of — but Slavery — free territory — & the Wilmot Proviso." The prominence of this issue threatened the stability of the bisectional coalitions that formed the backbones of both major parties. Any supporter of the principle of the Wilmot Proviso would be unacceptable to Southerners, and a candidate who openly took the view that slavery should be permitted in the territories would be equally unacceptable to Northerners. In May, seeking to find a middle ground acceptable to both sections, the

Democrats adopted a platform committing the party to the "principles and compromises of the Constitution" and nominated Lewis Cass of Michigan, the champion of "popular sovereignty" — the view that the people of each territory should be allowed to determine for themselves whether to allow slavery. The Whigs, on the other hand, sought to avoid taking any position on the issue, adopting no platform and nominating Mexican War hero General Zachary Taylor, a Louisiana slaveowner with no political track record whose views on the territorial issue were unknown. Dissatisfied with both candidates, in August a group of antislavery Democrats and Whigs from the North united to form the Free Soil Party and nominate Martin Van Buren on a platform that endorsed the principles of the Wilmot Proviso.

Against this background, on June 27, with the support of President Polk, Democratic Sen. Jesse Bright of Indiana proposed to extend the Missouri Compromise line to the Pacific Ocean. This proposal drew fire from both sides of the political spectrum. Antislavery Northerners continued to argue that slavery should be banned from all of the territory that had been acquired from Mexico. Conversely, while disclaiming any intention to actually introduce slavery into Oregon, some Southerners, such as Calhoun and Democratic Sen. Jefferson Davis of Mississippi, insisted that Congress had no constitutional authority to outlaw slavery in any of the territories. Nonetheless, most Southerners continued to support the principles underlying the Missouri Compromise. On August 11 the Senate voted 33-22 in favor of the extension of the Missouri Compromise line, with slave-state senators 25-2 in favor and free-state senators 20-8 against. The House of Representatives once again demurred, this time on a purely sectional vote. Finally, on August 12 the Senate agreed to organize a territorial government for Oregon with an explicit prohibition on slavery, as three Southerners joined the united Northerners to provide a 29-25 majority. On August 14 Polk signed the bill, noting that Oregon lay entirely north of the Missouri Compromise line. At long last, Oregonians had a territorial government.

The controversy over the organization of Oregon reflected the increasing sectional tension over the issue of slavery in the territories. In a very real sense, however, the dispute over Oregon was only a preliminary skirmish. A far more pivotal battle erupted the following year, after a group of Californians met in convention and sought to be admitted as a free state without passing through the stage in which they would be governed as a territory under legislation adopted by Congress. Their petition required Congress to once more directly confront the issues that had been raised by the Wilmot Proviso.

This crisis that ensued was in many ways parallel to the earlier dispute over the admission of Missouri. This time, however, it was the South that raised objections. Like the Northern opponents of the admission of Missouri thirty years earlier, Southerners argued that the admission of California would upset the balance of power in Congress, leaving them totally at the mercy of politicians from the other section of the nation. By 1849 Northerners had a clear majority in the House of Representatives, so Southerners viewed parity in the Senate as critical to the protection of their interests. The admission of California would give the free states a clear majority in the upper chamber as well. In addition, as Calhoun pointed out in his famous valedictory address in 1850, other potential free states were already in the pipeline, whereas no comparable slave states were on the horizon. Thus, the North would be in firm control of both branches of the legislature. A number of Southerners threatened to leave the Union rather than accept this state of affairs.

The solution proposed by the newly elected Whig President Zachary Taylor, himself a Louisiana slaveowner, did nothing to assuage Southern anxieties. Taylor suggested that both California and New Mexico — the southern portion of the Mexican Cession — should be admitted without first passing through the territorial stage. Most observers believed that under these circumstances, a state constitutional convention in New Mexico would also produce an antislavery constitution, but the South would at least avoid the indignity of a reprise of the struggle over the Wilmot Proviso. However, expressing dismay over what they saw as Northern intransigence in the disputes over the proviso and the organization of the Oregon territory, Southerners refused to accept Taylor's formulation.

The dynamic was further complicated by a dispute over the border between the state of Texas and the territory that had been recently acquired from Mexico. Southerners wished to maximize the size of Texas, which was safely designated as slave territory. Conversely, Northerners wished to have the disputed area included in the Mexican Cession, hoping that they could prevent slavery from being established there. This conflict exacerbated the tensions arising from the situation of California.

One solution to these problems might have been to adopt the same approach that had ultimately resolved the crisis of 1820. By extending the Missouri Compromise line to the Pacific (or at least to the border of California), Southerners would have been guaranteed hegemony over a part of the Mexican Cession, just as the original Missouri Compromise assured the free states of control of most of the Louisiana Purchase. While some Southerners continued to espouse this approach, the disputes of the 1840s had demonstrated that Northerners would no longer accept a formal territorial division. Indeed, many representatives of the free states had no interest in any compromise on the territorial issue. For example, Whig Sen. William H. Seward of New York pronounced any compromise "radically wrong and essentially vicious," and Whig Rep. Horace Mann of Massachusetts declared, "Better disunion, better a civil or servile war — better anything that God and his providence shall send — than an extension of the boundaries of slavery." Many Southerners were hardly less adamant. For example, noting that the North had rejected both the Missouri Compromise line and other proposed compromises in 1848, Democratic Rep. Winfield S. Featherston of Tennessee declared that "the South . . . has exhausted the cup of forbearance. . . . Her rights she is now . . . firmly resolved to demand and have, peaceably, constitutionally if she can; but forcibly, if driven to such a course." Against this background, secession by the Southern states loomed as a real possibility.

Ultimately, however, both sides stepped back from the brink. The framework for a settlement was initially created on January 29, 1850, by Sen. Henry Clay — the same man who had engineered the Missouri Compromise. Clay proposed a series of resolutions under which California would be admitted to the Union and Congress would create governments for the remainder of the Mexican Cession — the Utah and New Mexico territories — with no restriction on slavery. Texas would yield on the boundary issue, but it would be compensated by the assumption of its public debt by the federal government. Clay was supported by Whig luminaries such as Sen. Daniel Webster of Massachusetts and President Millard Fillmore of New York, who had become chief executive on July 10 after the death of Zachary Taylor.

Despite the support of such important figures, Clay's proposals were adopted only after an intense political struggle. Among Northern Whigs, Fillmore and Webster (who left the Senate to join Fillmore's cabinet) stood virtually alone in favoring a settlement on any terms other than those of the Wilmot Proviso. At the same time Southern Democrats continued to insist that at least the southernmost parts of the Mexican Cession be open to slavery. Initially, Clay presented his solution to the territorial issue as a single package, hoping that partisans on both sides of the dispute would be willing to sacrifice parts of their respective programs in order to reach a settlement. However, on July 31 an unusual coalition of Northern Whigs and Southern Democrats combined to sabotage this strategy, first eliminating the New Mexico territorial government provisions by votes of 33-22 and 28-25, next doing away with the Texas boundary settlement by a vote of 29-28, and at last dropping California statehood by a vote of 29-28. All that remained was a bill to organize the Utah territorial government without settling the issue of slavery. This bill passed the Senate by a vote of 32-18, as eleven Northern Democrats joined the united South in support.

At this point, Democratic Sen. Stephen A. Douglas of Illinois took charge of the compromise effort. Douglas chose to abandon the omnibus strategy in favor of treating each part of the proposed territorial settlement separately. This strategy proved successful. On August 9, with both sections and both parties divided, the Texas boundary bill was approved by a vote of 30-20. On August 13, four Southern Whigs and two Southern Democrats joined Northern senators to admit California on a vote of 34-18. Conversely, on August 15, the Senate, rejecting the views of six Northern Whigs, one Free Soiler, and three Northern Democrats, organized New Mexico on the same terms as Utah, with ten Northern Democrats and one Northern Whig joining sixteen Southern senators to create a margin of 17 (27-10). Though similarly divided, the House of Representatives followed suit, and the territorial provisions of the Compromise of 1850 became law.

In some respects, the dynamic that produced the resolution of the territorial issues in 1850 was the mirror image of that which ultimately led to a settlement of the Missouri controversy. In 1820 a handful of Northern congressmen had provided the margin by which Missouri was admitted without restriction on slavery. In 1850 six Southern senators voted with a unanimous North to admit California as a free state. To complete the bargain in 1820, a small majority of Southerners had joined their unanimous Northern colleagues to prohibit slavery north of the Missouri Compromise line. Similarly, as part of the compromise of 1850, substantial numbers of Northerners voted with the vast majority of Southerners to organize Utah and New Mexico without the Wilmot Proviso.

However, the Compromise of 1850 differed substantially from the Missouri Compromise in at least one critical respect. In 1820 Northerners had received an unequivocal promise that the territory north of 36 degrees, 30 minutes would be free from slavery. In 1850 the South received no such promise. Instead, the territories of Utah and New Mexico were organized without any resolution of their status as slave or free. To be sure, by 1850 most Southerners subscribed to the theory that slavery was legal in the territories in the absence of an express prohibition by the federal government. However, this view was controversial. The theory was particularly questionable when applied to the Mexican Cession, where slavery had been banned by the Mexican government at the time that the land was acquired by the United States. In any event, the situation in Utah and New Mexico was left far more ambiguous than that in the portion of the Louisiana Purchase that was north of the Missouri Compromise line.

The majority of Southern members of Congress were willing to accept this ambiguous state of affairs for a number of different reasons. First, as part of the compromise package, Congress moved toward the Southern position on the contentious issue of fugitive slaves. In the aftermath of *Prigg*, Southerners had become increasingly dismayed by the efforts of a number of Northern state legislatures to obstruct what Southerners viewed as the legitimate attempts of slaveowners to recover fugitive slaves. Southern anger was fueled further by the so-called McClintock Riot, in which a slaveowner was killed in Carlisle, Pennsylvania, during an effort to retrieve a runaway. The Fugitive Slave Act of 1850 addressed Southern concerns by providing slaveowners with a far more effective mechanism for the recovery of fugitives.

In addition, given the relative political strength of the two sections, congressional neutrality on slavery in the territories was the most that the South could hope to attain. Most Northern representatives and senators would have found the idea of affirmatively voting to establish slavery unthinkable. Instead, for Northerners, the choice was between adopting the principle of the Wilmot Proviso or saying nothing at all about slavery. Thus, Southerners who wished to resolve the crisis of 1850 without disrupting the Union were nothing more than political realists who saw little choice but to accept the terms offered for Utah and New Mexico.

The passage of the Compromise of 1850 was greeted with joy and relief by much of the nation. Many saw the compromise as finally resolving the divisive issues arising from slavery. For example, on December 18, 1851, Democratic Sen. Henry S. Foote of Mississippi asserted that it was "a definitive settlement of the disturbing question, which it proposes to adjust," and the following day Douglas himself declared "that I have determined never to make another speech on the slavery question." Ultimately, however, the hopes of men such as Foote and Douglas proved illusory. The Compromise of 1850 was not to be a final resolution of the sectional conflict but rather only a postponement of the ultimate reckoning.

The continued tension over slavery reflected the influence of a number of different forces. First, the acceptance of the compromise measures was hardly universal. For example, on December 16, Democratic Sen. Robert B. Rhett of South Carolina — a disciple of John C. Calhoun—assailed the compromise as "injurious to the South and . . . ultimately . . . destructive to our rights and liberties." Dissatisfaction was even more widespread among Northern Whigs. The depth of this dissatisfaction became apparent on April 5, 1852, when the House of Representatives considered a series of resolutions purporting to recognize the finality of the compromise measures. After a complicated series of roll-call votes, a finality resolution passed by a vote of 103-74. In votes on both final passage and the complicated procedural motions that preceded it, Southern Whigs supported the principle of finality almost unanimously, Southern Democrats evinced overwhelming support, and a solid majority of Northern Democrats also voted for the resolutions. However, Northern Whigs refused to endorse finality by a vote of 3-1. Similarly, at the Baltimore convention that chose Gen. Winfield Scott as the party candidate for president in 1852, sixty-six Northern Whigs refused to support a plank in the party platform that affirmed the finality of the settlement. Scott himself — a Virginian who was paradoxically the preferred candidate of the antislavery wing of the party — also refused to pledge fealty to the Compromise of 1850.

Scott's decision in particular had a significant impact on the structure of Southern politics. His reticence reinforced the impression that, although a Virginian himself, he was closely aligned with those Northern politicians who were unwilling to acquiesce in *any* concessions to the South on issues related to slavery. This impression led Southern Whigs to stay away from the polls in droves in 1852, contributing not only to the election of Democrat Franklin Pierce to the presidency but also to the defeat of Whig candidates for other offices. In the House of Representatives, Southern Whigs — often a force for compromise — held only twenty-two seats after the election. Those Southern Whigs who remained in Congress were acutely aware of the need to demonstrate to their constituents that they were reliable protectors of Southern interests.

Even those who supported the territorial provisions of the compromise disagreed on the import of those provisions. In particular, representatives of the two sections differed on the implications of congressional silence on the issue of slavery. Northern members of Congress believed that the Utah and New Mexico statutes embodied the principle of popular sovereignty, leaving territorial legislatures the option of banning slavery if they so chose. Thus, Douglas announced to his constituents in Chicago that the settlement recognized the "right" of territorial residents to regulate "their own internal concerns and domestic institutions in their own way." By contrast, Southerners such as Whig Sen. Robert Toombs of Georgia took the view that nonintervention implicitly authorized slaveholders to bring their slaves into the territories, declaring that the Utah and New Mexico bills "contained all [the South] did demand." Ultimately, however, it was a quite different issue that would unravel the short-lived peace achieved through the Compromise of 1850. The issue was the future of the Missouri Compromise.

In a purely formal sense, the repeal of the Missouri Compromise was simply not an issue in the struggle over the admission of California and the organization of the Utah and New Mexico territories. By their terms, each of the three bills dealing with these issues was territorially limited. Even a suggestion that any of the bills would alter the disposition of the lands of the Louisiana Purchase would have led to their demise. Indeed, the issue was not even discussed. Thus, subsequent claims by Southerners that the Compromise of 1850 by its terms implicitly repealed the Missouri Compromise are simply insupportable.

On another level, however, the Compromise of 1850 had a profound impact on the continuing effectiveness of the arrangements of 1820. The Missouri Compromise did not establish territorial governments in any of the areas north of 36 degrees, 30 minutes. Each such government required separate legislation that could, in theory at least, modify or abrogate the terms established by the compromise. At least in the Senate, Southern cooperation was needed to adopt the necessary legislation without such modifications. Prior to 1850, such cooperation was provided without incident.

The events of 1850 and the immediately preceding years dramatically changed the political dynamic. In the long struggle over the organization of Oregon and the Mexican Cession, Southern efforts to adopt the Missouri Compromise line as a general principle had been conclusively rejected. Southerners viewed this rejection as a repudiation of the basic understanding that had underlain both the Northwest Ordinance and the Missouri Compromise itself. Representatives of the slave states became even more acutely aware of the fact that if they continued to acquiesce in the organization of free states in the area of the Louisiana Purchase, they would soon find themselves at the mercy of the representatives of the free states. Many believed that the events in the years that culminated in the adoption of the Compromise of 1850 did not augur well for the consideration of Southern interests. Against this background, Southerners believed themselves absolved from any duty to cooperate in the organization of new territories from which slavery was excluded.

Initially, Southern reluctance to cooperate was expressed through a refusal to agree to the organization of the Nebraska Territory, which was located north of the Missouri Compromise line. In the House of Representatives, proponents of a territorial government were able to overwhelm Southern opposition in early 1853 and approve the Nebraska bill on a vote of 98-43. However, when Sen. Stephen Douglas introduced a similar bill in the Senate, it was tabled by a vote of 23-17 in March 1853, with Southern senators voting against Douglas by a margin of 17 (19-

2). Douglas nonetheless remained determined to organize the territory in order to secure a central route for the transcontinental railroad. Thus, he reintroduced the Nebraska bill in the Thirty-third Congress, unwittingly setting in motion the series of events that would ultimately destroy any hope of sectional harmony.

As the price for their support, Southerners insisted that the Nebraska bill repeal the Missouri Compromise. Douglas himself apparently would have preferred that slaves not come into the territories and believed that natural conditions would prevent slavery from taking hold west of the Mississippi. At the same time, he was sincerely committed to the principle of popular sovereignty and more concerned with obtaining the support necessary for the establishment of the territorial government. When he introduced the Nebraska bill on January 4, it did not specifically address the question of slavery but simply provided for the admission of states carved from the territory "with or without slavery, as their constitution shall prescribe at the time of their admission." Representatives of the slave states found this formulation unacceptable because it would have created a situation in which slaveowners could vote for a proslavery constitution but would have been barred from bringing slaves into the territory prior to the admission of the newly created states.

Douglas next proposed to add a clause that stated that "all questions pertaining to slavery in the Territories . . . are to be left to the people residing therein, through their appropriate representatives." Southerners remained unmollified, believing the prohibition of 1820 would have remained in effect until superseded by the actions of a territorial legislature that would presumably be elected without the influence of slaveowners, who would be unlikely to emigrate to the territory unless the ban on slavery was removed. Thus, on January 16 Kentucky Whig Archibald Dixon announced that he would offer an amendment that would not only repeal the prohibition on slavery in the Missouri Compromise but would explicitly empower slaveholders "to take and hold their slaves within any of the Territories of the United States." After consultations with both Dixon and Southern Democrats, Douglas responded by altering his bill so that, when finally reported to the Senate floor on January 23, 1854, it explicitly declared that the Missouri Compromise had been repealed by the Compromise of 1850 and was therefore "inoperative and void." The revised bill also split the newly organized territory into Kansas in the south and Nebraska in the north — a regime that was perceived widely as setting the stage for the ultimate admission of one slave state and one free state.

Not surprisingly, a fierce debate ensued. The supporters of the bill fell into two camps. Southerners railed against what they saw as the unjustness of the Missouri Compromise line. For example, Dixon asserted that the restriction that had been imposed in 1820 "tramples the great doctrine of equality of States underfoot, and tears asunder the chart upon which the liberty of the people is written." Other supporters saw the principle of popular sovereignty not only as right in itself but also as providing the best possibility for removing the question of slavery from national politics. Democratic Rep. Moses McDonald of Maine asserted that under popular sovereignty, "the question [of slavery] becomes local. No longer will there be any inducements, and most certainly no propriety, in discussing the question at the North, or in nonslaveholding communities."

The opponents of the bill were no less emphatic. Whig Rep. Aaron Harlan of Ohio complained that "the barricades and bars heretofore erected to obstruct the progress of slavery are to be broken down, and a great highway is to be opened up to facilitate its progress by the passage of [the] bill." In the Appeal of the Independent Democrats, a group of radical antislavery congressmen and senators was even more vehement, describing the Kansas-Nebraska bill as "a gross violation of a sacred pledge . . . a criminal betrayal of precious rights . . . part and parcel of an atrocious plot" to turn the territory into a "dreary region of despotism, inhabited by masters and slaves."

Despite such protests, Douglas and his allies were ultimately successful in driving the Kansas-Nebraska bill through Congress. In the Senate, the bill carried by a vote of 37-14, as fourteen Northern Democrats joined a near-unanimous South in defeating a polyglot alliance of seven Northern Whigs, four Northern Democrats, one Free Soiler, and two maverick Southerners. Resistance in the House of Representatives was much stiffer. For a time it seemed possible that Southern Whigs in the House would unite in voting against the bill. However, as Michael F. Holt has observed, the wide circulation of the Appeal of the Independent Democrats had raised the political cost of this course of action by associating opposition to the Kansas-Nebraska bill with the most radical antislavery elements in Northern politics. Against this background, with the support of Democratic President Franklin Pierce, the bill prevailed by a vote of 113-100. Sixty-nine of seventy-eight slave-state representatives voted for the bill, including seven of the nineteen Southern Whigs who voted. Half of the Northern Democrats in the House supported the Douglas bill as well. By contrast, Northern Whigs were unanimously opposed.

Prior to the Missouri Compromise, the principle of popular sovereignty had implicitly governed the entire Louisiana Purchase without creating great consternation in any of the territories. Against the background of the disputes of the 1840s and 1850s, application of the same principle proved a recipe for disaster. Representatives of both free states and slave states recruited settlers for Kansas, each group hoping to secure the territory for its camp. Violence between the two groups became commonplace, and in the first election for a territorial legislature Missourians crossed the border in droves to fraudulently cast votes for proslavery candidates. In short, rather than dampening sectional tensions, as its partisans had hoped, the move to popular sovereignty exacerbated the conflict between North and South.

The reaction of the national political system to the adoption of the Kansas-Nebraska Act was no less intense. Ironically, the repeal of the Missouri Compromise created the very sectional realignment of politics that had been sought by some of those who initially ignited the Missouri controversy. Already riven by sectional dissension over the passage of the Compromise of 1850 and shaken by a massive influx of immigrants who overwhelmingly supported the Democratic Party, the Whig Party disintegrated as a national organization after the events of 1854. At first it appeared that the Whigs might be replaced by an equally bisectional Know Nothing Party, organized around the principles of nativism. However, the nascent Know Nothings proved unable to effectively manage divisions over slavery, and by the time of the election of 1856 the party was competitive only in the South. In the North the major opposition to the Democrats came from a newly formed antislavery organization composed of refugees from the Whig Party, antislavery Democrats, and former members of the Free Soil Party: the Republican Party.

The Republicans were unique among the major political parties of the nineteenth century. The party was not only entirely sectional but largely defined the interests of the North negatively, by reference to what party members saw as the pernicious influence of what they described as the slave power. The specific issue that united the party was opposition to slavery in the territories. However, the ultimate goals of its leadership were much broader. While disclaiming any intention of interfering with slavery in existing states and pledging to observe the limits imposed by the Constitution, Republicans were openly hostile to the basic political, economic, and social structure of the South. As Don E. Fehrenbacher has observed, Republicans characterized the slaveholder "as a man who put on a show of chivalrous conduct, but underneath was cruel and cowardly, rendered brutal by the institution he cherished." Further, Republicans were determined to use all constitutional methods to purge the South of what they saw as the pathologies engendered by a slave-based economy and to instill in Southerners the virtues that characterized Northern society. In short, the Republican Party was not simply antislavery; it was, in a broader sense, anti-Southern.

Conversely, while maintaining its national character, the Democratic Party was increasingly dominated by Southern interests. On one hand, the Northern wing of the party was weakened by defections to the Republicans. On the other, the Southern wing was strengthened by the addition of some of the refugees from the defunct Whigs. Thus, the sectionalization of the national political process that had begun in the 1840s had greatly increased by the mid-1850s.

Seeking to preserve party unity, in 1856 the Democrats nominated James Buchanan of Pennsylvania for president on a platform that advocated "non-interference by Congress with slavery in state or territory," but took no position on the doctrine of popular sovereignty. However, the Republican message proved to be far more popular in the North. John Fremont of California, the Republican presidential candidate, was victorious in eleven of the nonslave states, whereas Democrat James Buchanan of Pennsylvania carried only five. Nonetheless, Buchanan triumphed in the election because of his overwhelming support in the slave states. In most of these states Fremont was not even on the ballot, and Buchanan lost only Maryland to Know Nothing candidate Millard Fillmore.

Moreover, both Southern Democrats and Republicans increasingly cast their positions on slavery in terms not only of political expediency but also of constitutional principle. The Southern position had been prefigured as early as 1819, when a number of Southerners argued that Congress lacked the authority to abolish slavery in the Arkansas Territory. By the mid–nineteenth century, proslavery constitutional theorists increasingly relied on two different arguments. The first began with the premise that, absent legislative prohibition, slavery would be legal in the territories, and that the Constitution nowhere granted Congress the power to outlaw slavery. The other argument was based on the view that the territories were the "common property" of the states, to which the citizens of all the states were entitled to equal access, and that the prohibition on slavery effectively denied the citizens of the Southern states such access.

By contrast, the Republican constitutional argument — developed largely by Salmon P. Chase — began with the basic principle first enunciated in *Somerset*, in which Lord Mansfield asserted that slavery was inconsistent with natural law and therefore could exist only where explicitly sanctioned by positive law. Reasoning from this premise, Chase contended that unless and until Congress or a territorial legislature acted, all erstwhile slaves brought into a territory automatically became free. He concluded that such a statute would deprive previously free people of their liberty without due process of law — a position that was embodied in the platforms of the Liberty Party, the Free Soil Party, and finally the Republican Party.

By the 1850s both proslavery and antislavery constitutional arguments were staples of the congressional debates over slavery in the territories. During the legislative process, the significance of these arguments was entirely rhetorical; one can hardly imagine them having any effect on actual votes. By contrast, constitutional arguments would almost by definition become of vital importance once the issue was joined in legal proceedings. Ironically, the case that brought those issues to the Supreme Court did not involve a resident of the territories at all. Instead, it was a dispute over the status of a black man and his family in the slave state of Missouri. The name of the case was *Dred Scott v. Sandford*.

CHAPTER 5

The Road to the Supreme Court

Sometime in the late eighteenth or early nineteenth century, Dred Scott was born enslaved to Peter Blow, the owner of an 860-acre farm in Virginia. Scott was a dark-skinned man who reportedly grew to slightly over five feet tall. In 1818 he moved with the Blow family to Alabama, where the Blows raised cotton, and in 1830 relocated with the family to Saint Louis, Missouri, where Peter Blow opened a boardinghouse. There Scott was sold to Dr. John Emerson. The circumstances of the sale are not entirely clear; some of the evidence indicates that the transaction was consummated by Peter Blow himself, but other sources suggest that Scott was sold by Blow's daughter, Elizabeth, shortly after Blow's death following a brief illness on June 23, 1832. In any event, the sale clearly took place sometime before the end of 1833.

Scott's new master was a physician who had been born in Pennsylvania in 1802 or 1803 and received his medical degree from the University of Pennsylvania in 1824. After apparently living for a time in the South, Emerson settled in Saint Louis sometime prior to August 1831. By September 1832, he had set his sights on a career as a medical officer in the army. On September 28, Emerson received his first opportunity to serve in the military after the army doctor stationed at the Jefferson Barracks, south of Saint Louis, became ill. Emerson was appointed to be the doctor's temporary replacement. Initially, the appointment was to last only one month, but Emerson in fact served in this capacity until June 5, 1833, when he was replaced by a regular army doctor.

Obtaining a permanent military position was more challenging for Emerson. With only about six thousand soldiers in the entire army, the demand for medical personnel was quite limited. Further, the appointments were distributed in proportion to a state's representation in Congress, and all of the positions allocated to Missouri were filled. Emerson, however, had powerful allies. He gained the written support of the commanding officer of Jefferson Barracks, thirteen members of the Missouri state legislature, and U.S. Senator Thomas Hart Benton of Missouri. Emerson was able to present himself as a candidate from Pennsylvania, and he was appointed assistant surgeon of the army on October 25, 1833. Accompanied by Dred Scott, on December 1, 1833, Emerson reported for duty at Fort Armstrong, which was located on Rock Island, in the middle of the Mississippi River, within the territorial boundaries of the state of Illinois.

There are no detailed accounts of Dred Scott's duties at Fort Armstrong during his stay there, but his master was clearly quite unhappy with his assignment. A physically decrepit facility located in a sparsely populated area, Fort Armstrong was clearly something less than a desirable posting. Within two months of his arrival, Dr. Emerson applied for a transfer, citing the need for treatment of a "syphiloid disease" that he had contracted in 1833. Although Emerson withdrew this request after his condition improved, within two years his influential friends were bombarding the War Department with letters requesting his transfer to the arsenal in Saint Louis. After being informed that such efforts at influence were inappropriate, Emerson apologized but then requested a transfer because of a "slight disease" in his left foot that might require surgery. After this request was denied, Emerson tried again, this time citing a quarrel with one of the company commanders as the reason he should be transferred.

Emerson finally was able to leave Fort Armstrong when the fort was vacated by the army in 1836. But unfortunately for him, he was transferred not to Saint Louis but to Fort Snelling in what was then the Wisconsin Territory, on the west bank of the Upper Mississippi near the subsequent site of Saint Paul, Minnesota. The fort was located in the territory acquired from France via the Louisiana Purchase, so slavery was prohibited there by the terms of the Missouri Compromise.

Accompanied by Dred Scott, Emerson arrived at Fort Snelling on May 8, 1836. While at Fort Snelling, Scott met Harriet Robinson, a much younger African American woman who was a slave to Major Lawrence Taliaferro, the local Indian agent. Dred and Harriet determined to marry and, unlike many other slaves who formed permanent relationships, solemnized their union in a formal civil ceremony some-time prior to September 14, 1837. Taliaferro, who was also a justice of the peace, presided over the ceremony. He then either gave or sold Harriet to Emerson.

While at Fort Snelling, Emerson continued to press for reassignment to a post in or near Saint Louis. He finally received the desired orders and left for Jefferson Barracks on October 20, 1837. However, because of the difficulty of travel conditions, Dred and Harriet Scott were left behind, with Emerson planning to send for them later. During this stage of Emerson's travels, Dred and Harriet were hired out to other people at Fort Snelling.

Unfortunately for Emerson, he was posted to Saint Louis for only a very short time. On November 22, he reported to his new assignment at Fort Jesup, Louisiana. There he met Eliza Irene Sanford, a Saint Louis woman who was visiting her sister, the wife of another officer who was stationed at the fort. After a very short courtship, John and Irene were married in Natchitoches, Louisiana, on February 6, 1838. Emerson sent for Dred and Harriet Scott, and they joined him at Fort Jesup in April 1838.

Despite his new marriage, Emerson was apparently even more unhappy at Fort Jesup than he had been at Fort Armstrong and Fort Snelling. Almost from the moment that he arrived in Louisiana, Emerson bombarded the surgeon general with requests for reassignment, citing dissatisfaction with the weather, problems with his health and his relationships with fellow officers, and a desire to be nearer Saint Louis in order to tend to his business affairs. Eventually Emerson persuaded the authorities to send him back to Fort Snelling, and John, Eliza, Dred, and Harriet departed Fort Jesup in September 1838. They landed in Saint Louis on September 21 and left Saint Louis on the steamer *Gipsey* on September 26, arriving at Fort Snelling on October 21. A child, Eliza, was born to the Scotts on the *Gipsey* while they were en route. Although historians have differed on the precise location of Eliza's birth, the weight of the evidence strongly suggests that Harriet gave birth when the steamer was north of the northern boundary of Missouri — once again, in territory in which slavery was forbidden by the Missouri Compromise.

The Emersons and Scotts remained together at Fort Snelling for more than a year and a half, when Dr. Emerson was ordered to Florida, where the Seminole War was being fought. They left Fort Snelling together on May 29, 1840, but Eliza Emerson did not accompany her husband to Florida. Instead, with the Scotts, she remained in Saint Louis, living with her father, Alexander Sanford. John Emerson remained in Florida until he was honorably discharged from the army in the fall of 1842. Although he continually made vigorous efforts to rejoin the military, Emerson was destined to spend the remainder of his life as a civilian. He returned briefly to Saint Louis and eventually moved with his wife to Davenport, Iowa, where he died on December 29, 1843.

The Scotts did not accompany the Emersons to Iowa. Instead they were apparently lent or hired out to the brother-in-law of Mrs. Emerson, Capt. Henry Bainbridge, who was stationed at Jefferson Barracks in 1842. Dred Scott at least may very well have accompanied Bainbridge when he was transferred first to Florida in 1843 and then to Fort Jesup in 1844 and Texas in 1845. In any event, all members of the Scott family were clearly in Saint Louis in March 1846, when Mrs. Emerson hired them out to Samuel Russell.

On April 6, 1846, Dred and Harriet Scott initiated *Dred Scott v. Emerson* and *Harriet Scott v. Emerson*, legal actions in the Missouri state circuit court in Saint Louis to establish their freedom. Following the standard model, the complaints were in form actions in trespass for assault and false imprisonment. For example, Dred Scott's complaint alleged that he was a free person held in slavery by Mrs. Emerson and that he was entitled to $10.00 damages because she had "beat, bruised and ill-treated" him and had falsely imprisoned him for twelve hours. The papers were initially filed on behalf of the Scotts by Francis B. Murdoch. However, as the state court action progressed, the Scotts were represented by a number of different attorneys. After Murdoch emigrated to California in 1847, he was replaced by Charles Daniel Drake. When Drake in turn moved to Cincinnati in June of that year, Samuel Mansfield Bay, formerly attorney general of Missouri, took on the suit. In July 1847 Alexander P. Field and David N. Hall entered the case; by March 1848 they had become the Scotts' sole legal representatives.

Mrs. Emerson's legal affairs were generally handled by Benoni S. Garland, the Sanford family attorney. To defend against the Scotts' suit for freedom, Garland retained George W. Goode, a native Virginian who was prominent in proslavery political circles. Goode handled the defense until 1849. He was replaced by Hugh A. Garland (no relation to Benoni) and his law partner, Lyman D. Norris. Garland and Norris were responsible for carrying the state action to its conclusion.

Based on existing Missouri law, the attorneys who represented Mrs. Emerson must have believed they faced an uphill struggle. In order to be successful in his suit for freedom, Scott had to prevail on two related but analytically distinct issues. He first had to demonstrate that during the course of his service in Illinois and the Wisconsin Territory, he had in fact become free under the law in force in either or both of those jurisdictions. He also had to show that he had remained free after his return to Missouri. On both of these issues, the law seemed to favor Scott at the time that he instituted his suit in state court.

British precedents provided the backdrop for the development of the American approach to both issues. In the 1772 decision in *Somerset v. Stewart*, a slave had been transported from Virginia to England, which had no legislation either establishing or prohibiting slavery. The slave escaped, only to be recaptured by his master, who then attempted to place him on a ship for the purpose of sending him to Jamaica for sale. Lord Mansfield issued a writ of habeas corpus ordering that the slave be released from the custody of the ship's captain, declaring famously that "the state of slavery is of such a nature that it is incapable of being introduced on any reasons, moral or political. . . . It is so odious that nothing can be suffered to support it but positive law."

Although Mansfield himself may have seen the decision in more limited terms, *Somerset* came to stand for the proposition that any slave who was brought into England gained his freedom at the moment that he entered the country. Moreover, as we have already seen, antislavery forces in America relied heavily on the language of the opinion in developing their constitutional theories. However, even given its broadest reading, *Somerset* did not speak to the status of a person who, having been free in England by operation of the law, returned to a jurisdiction in which slavery was legal. In 1826 the English High Court of Admiralty faced this issue in *The Slave, Grace*. In that case a slave accompanied her mistress to England but after a one-year visit returned voluntarily to Antigua. In rejecting the claim that the slave's sojourn in England prevented her reenslavement, Lord Sowell conceded that Grace had a right to freedom while in England.

Nonetheless, applying what was known as the doctrine of "reattachment," he concluded that this right "totally expired when that residence ceased and she was imported into Antigua" and that her "temporary freedom" was "superseded upon the return of the slave [to a jurisdiction where slavery was legal]."

Initially, neither the rule of *Somerset* nor *The Slave, Grace* found much favor in American courts. To be sure, unlike Lord Mansfield, Northern state judges had no need to rely on principles of natural law to conclude that the holding of slaves was not allowed within their jurisdictions. In the North, slavery was generally outlawed by statutes or constitutional provisions. Nonetheless, a number of different factors combined to help create a legal regime in which a slave did not automatically gain his freedom by virtue of his simple presence in a free state. First, the application of the *Somerset* principle to escaped slaves was flatly prohibited by the fugitive slave clause of the Constitution. In addition, although the Constitutional Convention had rebuffed the efforts of Charles Cotesworth Pinckney of South Carolina to provide additional protection for slave property in the privileges and immunities clause of Article IV, some Northern courts held that Southern slaveowners had a constitutional right to retain their slaves while passing through free states in transit between jurisdictions in which slavery was legal. Finally, Northerners were acutely aware of the need to balance their distaste for slavery with the needs of a federal system containing both free states and slave states. Thus, either by statute or judicial decision, the law of Northern jurisdictions often allowed Southerners to bring their slaves into a free state and to remain temporarily within that state without risking the slave gaining his freedom by operation of law.

The early Southern treatment of the doctrine of reattachment was often the mirror image of the Northern response to *Somerset*. Even by the terms of *The Slave, Grace*, the doctrine had no application in situations where the master and slave had become domiciled in free territory — that is, when the master had become a resident of such a territory with the intent to remain indefinitely. Southern courts often went even further, recognizing the freedom of erstwhile slaves even when they had been brought only temporarily into free states where they had become free by operation of the law of those states.

The legal regime gradually changed in the 1840s and 1850s. As antislavery sentiment intensified in the free states and sectional tensions rose, Northern state governments became increasingly likely to emancipate slaves who were temporarily within their jurisdiction. For example, in 1841 the New York state legislature repealed a law allowing masters to bring slaves into the state for up to nine months without risking emancipation, and in 1847 Pennsylvania repealed a similar law providing for a six-month grace period. By the late 1840s lower courts in both Ohio and Pennsylvania had even rejected the right of slave transit between two slave states, holding that even the most transient presence in those states emancipated a slave. Southern courts in turn became more sympathetic to the application of the doctrine of reattachment to African Americans who returned to slave states.

These trends were reflected in *Strader v. Graham*. In *Strader*, a Kentucky slaveowner had hired out three of his slaves to perform as musicians in Indiana and Ohio. After initially returning voluntarily to serve the master in Kentucky, the slaves escaped northward to Canada, first boarding a steamer that crossed the Ohio River into the state of Ohio. The master sued the owner of the steamship for damages in Kentucky state court under a statute that held owners liable for the value of escaped slaves under those circumstances. The owner of the steamboat based his defense on the ground that the escapees had in fact no longer been slaves because they had become free by the laws of Indiana and Ohio during their sojourns in those states and had remained free when they returned to Kentucky.

In 1847 the Supreme Court of Kentucky rejected this defense. The opinion reflected rising Southern anger over what Southerners viewed as disrespect from their Northern counterparts. While conceding that the laws of Indiana and Ohio had emancipated the slaves when they had been sent to those states to perform, the court observed that during their time in the free states, the slaves had been "sojourners for a transient purpose, not inhabitants or residents." Under these circumstances, the court asserted that to hold the escapees free under Kentucky law "would be carrying the principle of comity to an unwarrantable length," particularly since the free states had treated the Kentucky law on slavery "with so little respect." Citing *The Slave, Grace*, among other authorities, the court concluded that, under the facts of *Strader*, "a slave returning voluntarily with his master from a free State, is still a slave by the laws of his own country."

Strader, however, had not even been decided when Dred and Harriet Scott filed their suits for freedom in 1846. In any event, the decision was inconsistent with established principles of Missouri law. Although the Missouri courts had maintained that a master had a constitutional right to pass through free territories without losing dominion over his slave, they had also consistently held that residence in a free state for even a short period of time could effectively prevent the reattachment of the status of slavery when the former slave returned to Missouri. Moreover, in its 1836 decision in *Rachel v. Walker,* the state supreme court had held that Missouri would recognize the freedom of an African American under almost precisely the same situation presented by *Emerson* itself. In *Rachel* the court had concluded that the plaintiff had become free by virtue of the Northwest Ordinance and the Missouri Compromise when, in the course of the performance of his duties, an army officer had brought her to Fort Snelling, Minnesota, and Prairie Du Chien, Wisconsin, to be his servant, and that the doctrine of reattachment did not apply after the servant returned voluntarily with her master to Missouri.

Nonetheless, on November 19, 1846, Mrs. Emerson pleaded not guilty to the Scotts' complaint. Almost from its inception, the suit was beset by procedural complications. In order to prevail under Missouri law, a plaintiff in a suit for freedom was required to prove that he was held or claimed as a slave by the defendant — in this case, Mrs. Emerson. However, Samuel Russell — the witness on whose testimony the Scotts had hoped to rely to prove this point — ultimately admitted that he had no personal knowledge of any facts that would support such a conclusion. Faced with this lack of evidence, the jury returned a verdict for the defendant.

On July 1, 1847, Samuel Mansfield Bay, who had recently replaced Charles Drake as the attorney for the Scotts after Drake relocated to Cincinnati, moved for a new trial on the ground that the testimony of the witness had been a surprise and that Mrs. Emerson's claim of ownership could easily be proven. On the same date, Bay filed a new suit naming both Russell and Alexander Sanford as defendants in addition to Emerson, reasoning that Scott could prevail if any one of the three could be shown to have asserted a claim to him.

On July 31 the presiding judge ordered Scott's attorney to choose between the duplicate lawsuits, and the attorney chose to pursue the initial motion for a retrial. This motion was granted on December 2.

Mrs. Emerson's attorney promptly appealed this decision to the Missouri Supreme Court, but in June 1848 that court dismissed the appeal, holding that the grant of a new trial was not appealable because it was not a final judgment and clearing the way for a retrial of the Scotts' suit for freedom.

For reasons that have never been fully explained, the new trial was twice postponed and did not take place until January 12, 1850. At the new trial, Scott's counsel produced a new witness who testified that Mrs. Emerson had exercised dominion over Scott by hiring him out to Samuel Russell. The jury concluded that Scott should be declared a free man. Mrs. Emerson's attorney promptly appealed the judgment to the Missouri Supreme Court.

The appeal came to the court in the midst of the political upheaval that ultimately led to the adoption of the Compromise of 1850. In Missouri the dispute had exacerbated a split in the Democratic Party between the supporters and opponents of Democratic Sen. Thomas Hart Benton, the Van Burenite who had opposed the annexation of Texas and who alone among slave-state senators had consistently supported the principle of popular sovereignty during the long struggle over the fate of the Mexican Cession. Two of the three members of the Missouri Supreme Court in 1850— William B. Napton and James H. Birch — were strong supporters of the proslavery, anti-Benton faction of the party and may have seen in *Scott v. Emerson* an opportunity to strike a political blow at their adversaries. Birch at first favored an opinion that would have declared the restrictions on slavery in the Missouri Compromise unconstitutional. Napton, however, convinced him that the better course was simply to overturn the Missouri precedents rejecting the doctrine of reattachment and hold in favor of Mrs. Emerson on that more limited ground. Initially, John F. Ryland, the third member of the court, intended to dissent. Nonetheless, he ultimately agreed to concur in the conclusion that, after returning, both Dred and Harriet were slaves under Missouri law.

Despite all of this maneuvering, none of the three judges who initially heard *Scott v. Emerson* ever filed an opinion in the case. Although briefs were filed in March, the court deferred consideration of the appeal until its October term. The opinion was then assigned to Judge Napton, but he was unable to produce an opinion prior to the election of September 1851, in which new judges were elected to replace both him and Judge Birch. Thus, the case had to be reargued, and it was not until March 22, 1852, that the state supreme court finally handed down its ruling.

Judge Harry Gamble (who, ironically, had represented the army officer in *Rachel v. Walker*) concluded that the decision of the lower court should be affirmed. In Gamble's view, the case was governed by a straightforward application of the doctrine of *stare decisis*. Relying on *Rachel*, he declared, "I regard the question [presented in *Scott v. Emerson*] as settled by repeated adjudications of this court." Moreover, he observed that *Rachel* and similar cases had been decided "when the public mind was tranquil" and argued that the principles espoused by those cases had not been discredited in any way by subsequent events.

Judge Ryland joined the newly elected Judge William Scott in reaching a contrary conclusion. Speaking for the majority, Scott began by conceding that a variety of Missouri decisions had previously enforced the rules of nonslave states by recognizing the freedom of African Americans in positions similar to that of the Scotts. However, Judge Scott also observed that, however widespread the practice, the decision of one state to respect the internal laws of another state was entirely voluntary. He then complained, "It is a humiliating spectacle, to see the courts of this State confiscating the property of her own citizen by the command of a foreign law. If Scott is freed, by what means will it be effected, but by the constitution of Illinois, or the territorial laws of the United States? Now, what principle requires the interference of this court? Are not those governments capable of enforcing their own laws; and if they are not, are we concerned that such laws should be enforced, and that, too, at the cost of our own citizens?"

Later he adverted to the increasing political tensions between North and South: "Times are not as they were when [decisions such as *Rachel v. Walker*] were made. Since then not only individuals but States have been possessed with a dark and fell spirit with respect to slavery, whose gratification is sought in the pursuit of measures, whose inevitable consequence must be the destruction and overthrow of our government. Under such circumstances, it does not behoove the State of Missouri to show the least countenance to any measure which might gratify this spirit."

This inflammatory rhetoric provided the context for two more standard legal arguments. First, Judge Scott argued that the relevant portions of the Illinois constitution and the Missouri Compromise were penal laws and noted that penal laws were generally enforced only within the territorial limits of the jurisdictions in which they were adopted. In addition, citing *The Slave, Grace* and *Strader v. Graham,* he contended that the doctrine of reattachment applied in any event. Thus, Judge Scott concluded that Dred Scott and his family were not entitled to their freedom.

At this point, one might have thought that the logical next step for Dred Scott and his lawyers would have been to appeal to the Supreme Court of the United States. Such an appeal was never taken. Instead *Scott v. Emerson* was remanded to the lower court for a new trial, to be governed by the principles established by the state supreme court. However, the new trial was never held. Rather, almost two years later, an entry in the circuit court record for January 25, 1854, reported that *Scott v. Emerson* was "continued by consent, awaiting decision of Supreme Court of the United States." The decision to which the entry referred was an expected appeal from a separate action for freedom that had been filed on November 2, 1853, in the U.S. circuit court for the state of Missouri. Because the name of the defendant was misspelled, the action was styled *Dred Scott v. Sandford.*

The choice to file the new action rather than appeal the decision of the Missouri Supreme Court was made by Roswell M. Field, who had succeeded Alexander F. Field and David N. Hall as Scott's attorney. Field wrote privately that the reason he pursued this strategy was to circumvent what he saw as the implications of the Supreme Court's treatment of *Strader* when that case came to the Court on appeal from the Kentucky Supreme Court in 1851. In the *Strader* appeal the defendants had argued that the state of Kentucky was constitutionally required to recognize the freedom of the erstwhile slaves because they had become free under the laws of Ohio and Indiana, and that the same result was mandated by the antislavery provisions of the Northwest Ordinance. The Court in *Strader* unanimously held that it lacked jurisdiction over the appeal because neither claim presented a cognizable issue of federal law, concluding that "it was exclusively in the power of Kentucky to determine for itself whether [the slaves'] employment in another State should or should not make them free on their return," and that the Northwest Ordinance had lost the force of law in Ohio and Indiana when those states had been admitted to the Union. Field feared that the Court would take a similar view of an appeal from the decision of the Missouri Supreme Court in *Scott v. Emerson* and dismiss it for want of jurisdiction. Field wrote that he instituted the suit in federal court in the hope of eventually forcing the Court to a decision on the merits of the question of whether long-term residence in a free state or a territory in which slavery was prohibited by the Missouri Compromise established a claim to freedom that all states were required to honor.

To appreciate the rationale underlying this strategy, one must first understand the precise nature of the legal argument that Field and the other attorneys for the Scotts were making on behalf of their clients. None of the Scotts' lawyers ever contended in court that either the Constitution or a federal statute required the state of Missouri to recognize the freedom of slaves who resided in either a state where slavery was prohibited by state law or a federal territory where slavery was prohibited by the Missouri Compromise. Instead, the contention was that, as a matter of *common law*, the Scotts were entitled to their freedom under the circumstances of the case. As the Supreme Court had held in *Strader v. Graham*, the Court lacked authority to reverse a judgment on appeal from a state supreme court on these grounds. In such an appeal, the Court could only correct errors in federal law.

The posture of some cases initiated in federal trial courts was quite different. Under the Supreme Court's 1842 decision in *Swift v. Tyson*, in many common-law cases the federal courts were not required to apply the law of the state in which they were located. Instead, federal judges were to use their own best judgment in ascertaining the appropriate rule to be applied. Field hoped that the Supreme Court would ultimately reach a conclusion different from that of the Missouri Supreme Court on the question of whether African Americans in the position of the Scotts could retain their freedom after returning to a slave state.

In pursuing this strategy, Field was immediately confronted with a problem. The Constitution and the applicable statutes limit the types of cases that may be heard by the lower federal courts. The only conceivable basis for jurisdiction in the new federal case envisioned by Field would be diversity of citizenship — a claim that the plaintiff and the defendant were citizens of different states. Since both Dred Scott and Mrs. Emerson were residents of Missouri, a suit for freedom in federal court would have been dismissed immediately for want of jurisdiction. However, the complaint filed by Field in the federal court in Saint Louis alleged that title to Scott had been conveyed to John F. A. Sanford, the brother of Mrs. Emerson and the executor of Dr. Emerson's will. Sanford had recently moved to New York City and was therefore the resident of a different state than Dred Scott. The fortuity of this coincidence, together with the lack of a paper trail documenting the conveyance, has led some historians to conclude that the sale to Sanford in fact never took place and that he somehow colluded with Field to create the appearance of diversity of citizenship. But whatever the reality of the situation, Sanford admitted being the owner of Dred Scott, and this issue never became a subject of controversy in federal court.

By contrast, another aspect of the jurisdictional issue eventually took on central importance in the resolution of *Dred Scott*. Speaking for Sanford, on April 3, 1854, attorney Hugh Garland filed what was known as a plea in abatement, asserting that the court lacked jurisdiction because Scott was not a citizen. By its terms, this plea raised the question of whether African Americans were citizens who were entitled to invoke diversity jurisdiction under Article III of the Constitution.

Prior to *Dred Scott*, this question had rarely if ever been raised in diversity actions initiated by free blacks. Instead, the dispute over the constitutionality of the Negro Seamen's Acts had provided the backdrop for much of the debate about the citizenship of African Americans. Beginning in 1822, South Carolina and other Southern states had adopted statutes requiring that African American crew members of any ship coming into port be arrested and held in jail until their vessel departed, and that they be sold into slavery unless the captain of their ship paid the expenses incurred by the state for their room and board. The government of Massachusetts in particular had complained that African American crew members from that state were citizens of Massachusetts and that the application of the Negro Seamen's Acts to them denied them the rights guaranteed to them by the privileges and immunities clause of Article IV, often referred to as the comity clause.

The basic Southern defense of the constitutionality of the Negro Seamen's Acts rested on the contention that free blacks were not citizens under the Constitution and thus were not entitled to the protections of the comity clause. On this point Southern theorists relied on two analytically distinct arguments. Some used a state-centered theory of citizenship. They contended that national citizenship was derived from state citizenship, and that free blacks generally lacked the rights normally associated with citizenship in their home states and thus would not be considered citizens in those states. Other Southern theorists took a different view, asserting that citizenship for comity clause purposes was defined by national standards that excluded African Americans.

Neither approach was free from difficulty. First, any rights-focused definition of citizenship required the definition of a core set of rights that constituted the sine qua non of citizenship. Admittedly, many Northern states denied a wide variety of rights — particularly political rights — to their free black inhabitants. However, those same rights were also generally denied to women and children, who all conceded had the status of citizens under the Constitution. Indeed, in the antebellum era the most widely held view was that all free inhabitants who owed allegiance to a particular sovereign were citizens of that sovereignty. Under this definition, free blacks clearly qualified as citizens — a point recognized even by some slave-state courts in the early nineteenth century.

Further, even if one could specify a set of rights that were indispensable to citizenship, defining citizenship by reference to these rights would not have completely solved the Southern problem. The nature of the rights enjoyed by free blacks varied greatly even among the nonslave states. Although the legal regimes of states such as Indiana were almost as hostile to free blacks as those of the Southern states, a number of nonslave states allowed African Americans to vote even before the Civil War. Massachusetts also allowed free blacks to serve on juries. Thus, if the status of U.S. citizenship was derived from the possession of state-created rights, Southern theorists would have had to concede that at least *some* free blacks could claim the protection of the comity clause.

Finally, any state-centered approach to federal citizenship had to contend with troubling structural anomalies. By its nature, the constitutional definition of citizenship had only limited significance under the antebellum regime. It had no impact on purely domestic issues — most notably the relationship between a state and its own citizens. Thus, no definition of federal citizenship could threaten core principles of state autonomy. Instead, what was at stake was the enjoyment of some of the specific rights entrusted to the federal government by the Constitution. To have state governments control access to these rights necessarily created some tension with the basic idea that the federal government was supreme within the sphere of influence allocated to it by the Constitution.

The argument that federal citizenship might be defined independently from state citizenship faced different problems. By their terms, the wording of both the comity clause and the diversity of citizenship clause appear to be inconsistent with the notion that a person who is recognized as a citizen by his home state might not be considered a citizen for constitutional purposes. Neither clause refers to citizens of the United States per se. Instead, the comity clause provides that "the Citizens of *each State* shall be entitled to all Privileges and Immunities of Citizens in the several States," while the diversity clause vests the federal courts with jurisdiction to hear cases "between Citizens *of different States*" (emphasis added). These complex theoretical problems provided the background for the consideration of Garland's plea in abatement.

The plea was not skillfully drafted. It did not allege that Scott had remained a slave or had been born a slave. Nor did Garland specify the state in which Scott had been born. Instead, the plea asserted only that because Scott was a descendant of African American slaves, he could not be considered a citizen of the state of Missouri for purposes of diversity jurisdiction. These omissions helped shape the arguments on citizenship in both the circuit court and subsequent proceedings in the Supreme Court.

On April 14 Field demurred to the plea, effectively contending that the complaint in the case alleged facts sufficient to support the exercise of jurisdiction. When the issue was argued on April 24, Garland cited a number of cases that held that free African Americans were not citizens for purposes of the comity clause He contended that the principles animating these decisions applied equally to the Article III, Section 2 concept of diversity of citizenship for jurisdictional purposes. Field, by contrast, observed that African Americans had all the rights of citizens in *some* states and that, in any event, citizenship for Article III purposes required no more than simple residence.

The following day, presiding Judge Robert W. Wells, a slaveholder who at one point had been the attorney general of the state of Missouri, sustained the demurrer, finding that the plea in abatement presented insufficient grounds for dismissing the complaint. Wells argued that one need not qualify as a citizen for purposes of Article IV in order to qualify for diversity jurisdiction under Article III. In Wells's view, for purposes of the latter provision, one need be no more than a resident with the capacity to own property. Otherwise, he observed, a free African American would not only be unable to avail himself of diversity jurisdiction as a *plaintiff* but would also be immune from the exercise of such jurisdiction over him as a *defendant*. Unwilling to countenance this conclusion, Judge Wells found that the court had jurisdiction over the claims of Dred Scott and his family.

Having lost on the jurisdictional issue, Sanford's attorney defended the case on the merits. Field and Garland agreed on a statement of facts that, although not entirely accurate, conveyed the sense of the travels of Dred Scott and his family with Dr. Emerson and described the later conveyance of Scott to John Sanford. No additional witnesses or evidence were introduced at the brief jury trial that was held on May 15. At that trial Field argued that Scott was free by virtue of the operation of the Northwest Ordinance, the constitution of Illinois, and the Missouri Compromise. Conversely, Garland's argument tracked the reasoning of the Missouri Supreme Court in *Scott v. Emerson*. Believing himself bound by that case and the Supreme Court's decision in *Strader v. Graham*, Judge Wells charged the jury that the law was with Sanford, and the jury quickly returned a verdict in his favor.

This decision was in a very real sense only preliminary. From the moment that the case was filed in the circuit court, it was no doubt clear to all of the parties that *Dred Scott* would find its way to the Supreme Court. After his motion for a new trial was denied, Field filed an appeal with the Court on December 30, 1854. Although a crowded docket delayed consideration of the case for more than a year, the fate of Dred Scott and his family would ultimately be decided by the nine justices in Washington, D.C.

The Supreme Court in 1856

The Court that heard arguments on the *Dred Scott* case in 1856 differed substantially from that which had considered *The Amistad*, *Groves v. Slaughter*, and *Prigg v. Pennsylvania* in the early 1840s. In part the differences reflected changes in personnel: Four of the nine justices who would consider *Dred Scott* had taken their seats after *Prigg* was decided. In addition, the near-continuous sectional conflict had had a substantial impact on the views of even those justices who had been on the Court when *The Amistad*, *Groves*, and *Prigg* were decided.

The custom of choosing one member of the Court from each circuit guaranteed a large measure of geographical diversity among the justices. Thus, five were residents of slave states, and four resided in the North. However, in political terms, the *Dred Scott* Court was wildly unbalanced. Because of the vagaries of the appointment process and the fact that Democrats had occupied the White House for most of the Jacksonian era, in 1856 the Court was dominated by Democratic appointees. Four of the justices had been appointed by Andrew Jackson himself, and one each by Martin Van Buren, James K. Polk, and Franklin Pierce. Whig Millard Fillmore had also appointed one of the justices, as had the politically ambiguous John Tyler.

The leader of the Court in 1856 was Chief Justice Roger Brooke Taney. Taney was born on a large plantation in Calvert County on the Eastern Shore of Maryland on March 17, 1777. He received his early education from local schools and private tutors before entering Dickinson College in Carlisle, Pennsylvania, in 1792. Taney graduated from Dickinson in 1795 and was selected by his fellow students to give the valedictory address at the graduation ceremonies.

In 1796 Taney moved to Annapolis, Maryland. After reading law under the tutelage of Jeremiah Townley Chase, a local judge, Taney was admitted to the bar in 1799. He returned to Calvert County that same year and at the age of twenty-two was elected to the state House of Delegates as a Federalist, serving one term before being defeated in his bid for reelection in 1801. He made an unsuccessful bid to return to the House of Delegates in 1803 but in 1816 was selected to serve a five-year term in the state Senate. Taney left the legislature in 1821 and spent much of the 1820s establishing himself in Baltimore as a leading figure in the Maryland bar. He was selected to be the attorney general of the state of Maryland in 1827.

After the collapse of the Federalist Party, Taney aligned himself politically with Andrew Jackson in the early 1820s. He supported Jackson's unsuccessful presidential bid in 1824 and in 1828 played a leading role in the organization of the Jackson forces in the state of Maryland. In 1831 Jackson appointed Taney to be attorney general of the United States.

Taney's service in the cabinet was marked by his militant opposition to the Bank of the United States. In 1832 Congress passed a measure that would have renewed the bank's charter. Although a number of other cabinet members believed that Jackson should have signed the bill, Taney successfully urged a veto. After Secretary of the Treasury William J. Dunne refused to withdraw federal funds from the bank in September 1833, Jackson removed Dunne and appointed Taney to replace him. However, knowing that the supporters of the bank would oppose the nomination, Jackson did not send Taney's name to the Senate for confirmation until June 1834. Thus, although the Senate ultimately rejected his nomination on June 24, in the interim Taney succeeded in removing the funds and transferring them to state banks.

In January 1835 Gabriel Duvall of Maryland resigned from the Supreme Court. Jackson immediately appointed Taney to succeed him. Taney's enemies worked indirectly against the nomination by proposing a plan that would have merged the states of Maryland and Delaware into the Third Circuit and created a new circuit in the West. By custom, each circuit was represented on the Court by one of its residents; thus, if adopted, the plan would have effectively eliminated Taney from consideration. Although the measure was not adopted, it served the purpose of delaying the nomination until Congress had adjourned, thereby effectively killing it.

Taney's enemies had good reason to regret this success after Chief Justice John Marshall died on July 6, 1835. On December 28, 1835,

Jackson nominated Taney to replace him. By this time the political winds had shifted, and the administration had enough support in the Senate to secure confirmation. Thus, on March 15, 1836, Roger Brooke Taney succeeded to Marshall's position on the Court.

The views of the newly appointed chief justice on issues related to slavery seem to have hardened considerably as he aged. Taney had apparently shown some sympathy to the plight of slaves and free blacks during his tenure in the Maryland state legislature. Moreover, in 1818 he had vigorously and successfully defended the free-speech rights of a Methodist minister charged with attempting to incite slaves by delivering an abolitionist sermon in Hagerstown, Maryland. However, in 1832, in his capacity as attorney general of the United States, Taney prepared a strongly worded opinion defending the legality of the Negro Seamen's Act of South Carolina, denying that free blacks were citizens of the United States at the time of the drafting of the Constitution and describing African Americans generally as "separate and degraded people to whom the sovereignty of each state might accord or withhold such privileges as they deemed proper." Although the opinion was never published, it not only presaged Taney's treatment of the citizenship issue in *Dred Scott* but also reflected a powerful commitment to Southern ideology on constitutional issues related to slavery more generally.

The strength of this commitment was apparent in Taney's approach to *Prigg*. While joining Justice Story in concluding that Congress had authority to pass legislation enforcing the fugitive slave clause, Taney rejected the view that federal enforcement power was exclusive, arguing instead that states retained concurrent authority to aid slaveowners in the recovery of fugitives. Moreover, he stood alone on the Court in arguing that the Constitution *required* states to adopt such legislation. These arguments can only be seen as a reflection of Taney's attitude toward slavery and what he viewed as its special place in the constitutional scheme. The same attitude would be apparent in his treatment of the issues presented by *Dred Scott*.

When *Dred Scott* came to the Court, Associate Justice Peter Vivian Daniel was perhaps even more committed to the institution of slavery than Taney himself. Daniel was born on April 24, 1784, on a family farm in Stafford County, Virginia, an agricultural region approximately fifty miles south of Washington, D.C., and sixty miles north of Richmond. He received his early education from private tutors and in 1802 spent a few months at Princeton before returning to Stafford County. In 1805 Daniel moved to Richmond to study law in the offices of Edmund Randolph, a former aide to George Washington who had served as both attorney general and governor of Virginia and had also represented Virginia in both the Continental Congress and the Constitutional Convention. After being admitted to the bar in 1808, Daniel returned to Stafford County to practice. In 1809 he returned to Richmond as a representative to the state legislature and in 1810 married Randolph's younger daughter, Lucy. Soon thereafter, Daniel permanently relocated to Richmond.

The son-in-law and protégé of Edmund Randolph had immediate access to the highest circles in Virginia Democratic politics. He quickly became a prominent member of the so-called Richmond Junto, a network of influential Democrats that dominated Virginia politics for much of the first part of the nineteenth century. In 1824 the junto threw its support behind William H. Crawford of Georgia for president; ultimately the election was decided by the House of Representatives, and both Crawford and Andrew Jackson were defeated by John Quincy Adams. In 1828 Daniel vigorously supported the ticket of Jackson and John C. Calhoun of South Carolina and was rewarded as the Jackson-Calhoun forces carried Virginia and thwarted Adams's bid for reelection. When Jackson and Calhoun became rivals, Daniel threw in his lot with Jackson. Thereafter, until he assumed a place on the bench, Daniel was a loyal ally of the Jacksonian forces, helping to lead the battle against both Whigs and Calhounite extremists.

When Roger Brooke Taney left his position as attorney general to assume the position of secretary of the treasury, Daniel was Jackson's choice to be Taney's replacement. Daniel refused this appointment for financial reasons. However, in March 1836, when Philip P. Barbour left the federal district court for the eastern district of Virginia to become an associate justice of the Supreme Court, Daniel accepted an appointment to be his successor.

Although Daniel had great admiration for Jackson, he had a much closer personal relationship with Martin Van Buren, who was Jackson's trusted lieutenant. In the early 1820s Van Buren had established a political alliance between his Albany Regency and the Richmond Junto, and for more than two decades thereafter Daniel maintained an active correspondence with the "Little Magician," strongly supporting his campaign for the vice presidency in 1832 and the presidency in 1836. Thus, when Barbour died in office on February 25, 1841, it was entirely natural for Van Buren to choose Daniel as Barbour's successor. Daniel was confirmed after a brief but intense political struggle. The dispute over slavery that would soon become so prominent played no role in the struggle. Instead, the battle over Daniel's confirmation was simply a typical episode in the ongoing contest for political power between the Democrats and the Whigs.

Van Buren soon reported to Jackson that in nominating Daniel, he had taken the opportunity "to put a man on the bench of the Supreme Court . . . who will I am sure stick to the true principles of the constitution, and being a Democrat *ab ovo* [literally, "from the egg"] is not in so much danger of a falling off in the true spirit." In many respects, the tall, spare, dark-complected Daniel met or even exceeded Van Buren's expectations. A true agrarian conservative, Daniel was deeply committed to the constitutional theories embodied in the work of John Taylor and the Virginia and Kentucky Resolutions, which in 1798 had enunciated a strong theory of states' rights. Daniel viewed the defense of these principles against the advocates of the nationalist, probusiness policies associated with the Whig Party as an apocalyptic struggle between good and evil.

The strength of Daniel's convictions was reflected in the tone of his rhetoric. His public comments on politics were notable for their forcefulness; he was described by one political opponent as "one of the most violent partisan writers in the state." Daniel was no less emphatic in private. For example, in an 1832 letter to Van Buren, he described the forthcoming election as a "great struggle between democracy and the constitution on the one hand, and corruption and profligacy unexampled on the other" and declared that "the conflict we are now waging [is] against that worst of all influences; that which puts intelligence, probity, patriotism, falsehood, venality, vice in every form, all upon an equality, that is, values them merely as they can become means to be wielded to its purposes — *the influence of money*." Similarly, after meeting Daniel Webster, Daniel reported on one occasion that "my hand was actually contaminated with his." In short, as John P. Frank has aptly observed, "the Daniel who came to the Court in 1841 . . . was a man of controversy, ferocious, unyielding, and utterly humorless in dispute."

These attitudes and personal characteristics shaped Daniel's treatment of the constitutional issues that came before the Taney Court. Not surprisingly, the chief justice was Daniel's closest friend and ideological ally on the Court; however, Daniel was considerably more uncompromising than Taney in his positions on issues such as federalism and the rights of corporations. Thus, he dissented alone more than twice as often as any other justice during his tenure and more than three times as often as Taney, John Catron, and John A. Campbell combined.

One of the most notable features of Daniel's jurisprudence was his opposition to the expansion of federal power. On a wide of variety of issues, ranging from the interpretation of the commerce power to questions of federal jurisdiction, Daniel consistently argued that the authority of the federal government should be circumscribed within narrow limits. However, he was at times willing to subordinate this principle to the need to protect Southern interests; thus, in *Prigg*, Daniel announced his willingness to concur in the view that Congress had not exceeded its authority in passing the Fugitive Slave Act of 1793.

On the issue of federal exclusivity, however, Daniel's position was far more consistent with the overall pattern of his jurisprudence. Unlike Story, he concluded that, although Congress possessed the authority to implement the fugitive slave clause, states also retained power to pass laws that would provide further aid to the slaveowner. Most of his opinion in *Prigg* is devoted to a systematic canvass of the authorities that, Daniel contended, supported the theory of concurrent power in general terms. However, Daniel also emphasized the symbolic effect of a holding of federal exclusivity in the specific context of the fugitive slave clause and strongly endorsed the adoption of supplementary state legislation. Taken as a whole, the opinion reflects the views of a Southerner who, while obviously concerned with the defense of slavery, remained committed to the basic principles of legal discourse and hopeful of sectional accommodation.

By 1856, however, Daniel had become, in Fehrenbacher's words, a "brooding proslavery fanatic" whose mind was "completely closed on the slavery issue." Despite his unyielding personality, prior to 1847

Daniel would have been an unlikely candidate to become the standard-bearer for Southern extremism. Daniel's political alliance with Martin Van Buren was a model of bisectional cooperation, and his opinion in *Prigg*, though undoubtedly pro-Southern, was fairly moderate in tone. Moreover, Daniel was one of the few Southerners who opposed the movement for the annexation of Texas, viewing the campaign as a Calhounite conspiracy.

The dispute over the Wilmot Proviso was the event that transformed Daniel's political worldview. As early as 1845, Daniel had privately expressed the opinion that federal legislation explicitly limiting the right of slaveowners to bring slaves into the territories would be grounds for secession. At the same time, he evinced a willingness to accept the general idea of geographical division as a workable compromise. Two years later the New York State Democratic Convention adopted a resolution supporting the position that slavery should be outlawed in all of the territory that had been obtained from Mexico. Daniel then wrote to Van Buren seeking clarification of his position on this issue. When Van Buren replied evasively, Daniel (whose wife had recently died from a stroke) responded that if Van Buren in fact supported the Wilmot Proviso, "I shall have lived to witness a development that even the great and overwhelming and stunning calamity that has come upon me cannot prevent me from contemplating with deep sorrow and alarm. I shall have been constrained to perceive on the part of those, on whom of all the public men in this nation I imposed the greatest trust, what my deliberate convictions compel me to view as the overthrow of the great national compact; as the extreme of injury and oppression in its most galling form, because it declares to me that I am not regarded as an equal." Daniel's mortification can only have been magnified in 1848, when Van Buren became the presidential candidate of the Free Soil Party.

The impact of Daniel's sense of personal betrayal on the subsequent evolution of his political thought cannot be reliably assessed. What is clear is that, beginning in the late 1840s, Daniel associated all things Northern with the antislavery movement and hated the North with an obsessive fury that he had hitherto reserved for his Whig political enemies. He refused even to venture north of the Delaware River and became indifferent to the preservation of the Union. The intensity of his commitment to Southern institutions and interests shaped Daniel's approach to *Dred Scott*.

The most junior of the Southern justices in 1856 was John Archibald Campbell — the only one of the five who had not participated in *Prigg*. Campbell was born on June 24, 1811, the first child of a prominent family that owned a plantation in Wilkes County, Georgia. It became clear at an early age that Campbell was intellectually gifted. Thus, at the age of eleven, after only one year at the local school, he was sent to study in Athens, Georgia. There he attended a grammar school for one year before entering Franklin College in 1823, graduating in June 1925 with the first honors in his class. After financial difficulties forced him to abandon his dream of a military career, Campbell decided to become a lawyer.

In January 1829 Campbell moved to Saint Andrews, Florida, to read law with his uncle John Clark. Campbell rapidly completed his studies and returned to Georgia, where he was admitted to the bar at the age of eighteen. Seeking better career opportunities, Campbell relocated in March 1830 to Montgomery, Alabama, where he soon established a reputation as one of the ablest lawyers in the state. In both 1836 and 1852 Campbell was offered positions on the Alabama Supreme Court. In both cases he declined.

When Justice John McKinley died on July 19, 1852, the slavery issue played a significant role in determining his successor. President Millard Fillmore's nomination of Sen. George E. Badger of North Carolina was defeated in part because Badger had supported the Wilmot Proviso. Fillmore ultimately was unsuccessful in his effort to fill the seat before he was succeeded in the presidency by Franklin Pierce. After taking office as president, Pierce chose Campbell to succeed McKinley on the joint recommendation of Democratic Justice John Catron of Tennessee and Whig Justice Benjamin Robbins Curtis of Massachusetts.

The recommendation of the two sitting justices reflected the uniformly held opinion of Campbell's legal talents. One newspaper compared him favorably with Joseph Story, and even a publication that strongly disagreed with Campbell's political views conceded that "he is chock full of talent, genius, industry and energy. . . . For the last ten years, he has been deservedly at the head of the Alabama Bar . . .

exceedingly popular, and as a jurist and a man commands the respect and confidence of everyone." Nonetheless, the issue of slavery created some controversy. Unlike the concerns regarding the Badger nomination, the misgivings about Campbell were voiced by Northern antislavery Whigs.

The source of these misgivings was the ideological and legal positions that Campbell had expressed both publicly and privately in the years immediately preceding his nomination to the Court. Although his background and temperament differed significantly from those of Peter Daniel, Campbell was no less committed to the protection of Southern interests. Indeed, unlike Daniel and Taney, who were conventional Jacksonian Democrats at the time that they were nominated to serve on the Court, Campbell was a self-identified "Southern man," whose loyalty to sectional interests dominated his political worldview. He feared that many Northern Democratic politicians would seek to capitalize on rising antislavery sentiment to advance their personal careers. Thus, in the run-up to the elections of 1848, Campbell professed "indifference to the election of any Democrat [from] north of the Potomac" and believed that Zachary Taylor — a Whig — was the best available presidential candidate because Campbell hoped that Taylor, as a Southern slaveholder, would be more sympathetic to Southern interests.

In addition, Campbell was alarmed by the possible implications of the Mexican War. He opposed territorial acquisitions from Mexico, believing that, because the land was unsuitable for exploitation through slave labor, such acquisitions would inevitably destabilize the balance of power in favor of the North. Recognizing that territorial expansion was probably inevitable, as a second choice Campbell believed that either the treaty of cession or congressional action should guarantee slaveowners the right to bring their slaves into any newly acquired territory. Thus, in a letter to Calhoun, he opined that "slavery is the central point about which Southern Society is formed. It was so understood at the formation of the Constitution. It has been dealt with by the country since in the same spirit. This territory is the fruit of common expenditure and toil. We *must* insist that for the future the same spirit shall be maintained. We *must* have an organization of the territory that admits us as equals." At the same time, in 1848 Campbell privately expressed the view that Congress was not required by the Constitution to allow slavery in the territories; he simply contended that slavery should be allowed as a matter of policy.

Campbell's legal thought appears to have been radicalized by the crisis of 1850. As a delegate to the Nashville Convention of 1850, he drafted the resolutions that embraced the common property doctrine and declared that "every act of the federal government which places any portion of the property lawfully held in the States of the Union out of the protection of the federal government, or which discriminates in the nature and extent of the protection to be given to different species of property, or which impairs the title of the citizen in any of the territories of the Union, without affording just compensation, is a plain and palpable violation of the obligations of the government, and is contrary to the spirit and meaning of the constitution of the United States."

"The Rights of the Slave States," published in 1851, provides a more complete exposition of Campbell's views on the sectional conflict. There Campbell argued that the most important danger to the South lay in what he viewed as the rising tide of abolition in the North, contending that "the abolition of the slave trade and slavery in the District of Columbia, the Missouri and Oregon restrictions, and the dishonest settlement of the questions in regard to the Mexican conquests, are of themselves nothing, compared with the engrossing and pervading evil of antislavery agitation." Nonetheless, while observing that he would have "greatly preferred another field for the contest," he also asserted that the struggle over slavery in the territories acquired in the Mexican War "necessarily involved the fate of our institutions." Campbell decried the refusal of the North to recognize the principle that "slavery, as an institution of property, in the States, [is] entitled to the same rank, privilege and protection as every other institution of property" and declared that "the experiment of the fugitive slaves evinces that [Northerners] cannot fulfill their duties under the Constitution." Finally, in addition to calling for Southern unity, Campbell strongly defended the right to secession, asserting that "the union of twenty willing States, and eleven reluctant or subjugated ones, would be such a commentary upon our principles of self-government, that [not even committed Whigs] could endure the hideous record."

Antislavery politicians were understandably chagrined by Campbell's expression of such sentiments. However, even if they had been determined to oppose a Supreme Court nominee with such sterling credentials, they lacked the political power to block confirmation in the Senate. Thus, the opponents of slavery could only cling to the hope expressed by the *New York Times:* "Past experience has shown that, once placed [on the Supreme Court] for life, the professions of the partisan soon give place to the convictions and sense of high responsibilities of the jurist. . . . [James Moore Wayne and John McLean], the highest-toned federalists on the Bench have been taken from the Democratic ranks, and it will be strange if the views of a gentleman of first-rate legal talent, like Mr. Campbell should prove less conservative."

Even in 1853, with respect to slavery-related issues this prediction rested more on hope than on logic. Campbell was indeed deeply committed to the conventions of legal analysis. At the same time, he was equally committed to a constitutional theory that protected the rights of the Southern states in general and slaveowners in particular. Further, he believed that this constitutional theory was entirely consistent with the basic principles of legal analysis. By 1856 Campbell's attachment to these views can only have been strengthened by the bitter dispute over the Kansas-Nebraska Act and the meteoric rise of the Republican Party.

To be sure, as a judge Campbell did not uniformly support the more radical elements of the proslavery movement. For example, sitting on circuit in New Orleans in 1854, he had vigorously attacked "filibustering" expeditions designed in part to add slaveholding territories such as Cuba to the United States. In his charge to the jury, Campbell harshly criticized these expeditions as violative of the neutrality laws and reminded Southerners that Northerners could only be expected to fulfill their obligations under the fugitive slave laws if Southerners in turn lived up to their obligations under federal law. However, on the core issue of slavery in the territories, a committed Southern sectionalist such as Campbell was inevitably drawn to the position that the Constitution protected Southern rights.

While differing with Taney, Daniel, and Campbell on some issues of judicial philosophy, James Moore Wayne was also committed to the defense of slavery and Southern political interests more generally. Moore was born in 1790, the twelfth of thirteen children of a prominent Savannah, Georgia, planter, businessman, and slave trader. Wayne received his early education from a private tutor before attending the

College of New Jersey (the forerunner of Princeton University) and graduating with a bachelor of arts degree in 1808. From 1809 to 1810 he studied law with Judge Charles Chauncy in New Haven, Connecticut, and was admitted to the bar upon his return to Savannah in 1811. In 1815 Wayne entered politics, serving as a member of the state legislature and a state judge before being elected to the U.S. House of Representatives in 1828.

Although he had earlier been an ardent supporter of the presidential ambitions of William Crawford, by 1828 Wayne was a committed Jacksonian. As a member of the House, he earned the gratitude of both Jackson and Martin Van Buren with his vigorous denunciation of the nullification movement and leadership in the campaign against the Bank of the United States. When Justice William Johnson of South Carolina died in office in the summer of 1834, Jackson turned to Wayne to be his replacement. Although the Senate was dominated by Whigs, they no doubt understood that Jackson was unlikely to appoint any person whose views were more acceptable to them. Thus, Wayne was confirmed without great difficulty and sworn in on January 14, 1835—the first justice of the Supreme Court to have been born under the Constitution.

During his tenure on the Court, Wayne became known as a strong proponent of national power. This aspect of his political and jurisprudential philosophy was clearly on display in *Prigg*, in which he delivered a long opinion defending his decision to concur "altogether" with Story. The centerpiece of Wayne's argument was his claim that federal exclusivity was necessary to minimize the sectional friction created by the issue of fugitive slaves. He began by contending that

> The obligation [created by the fugitive slave clause] is common to all [the states] to the same extent. . . . Shall, then, each state be permitted to legislate in its own way, according to its own judgment, and their separate notions, in what manner the obligation shall be discharged to those states to which it is due? To permit some of the states to say to the others, how the property included in the provision was to be secured by legislation, without the assent of the latter, would certainly be, to destroy the equality and force of the guarantee, and the equality of the states by which it was made. . . . Is it not more reasonable to infer that [the states] meant that the

right for which some of the states stipulated, and to which all acceded, should, from the peculiar nature of the property in which some of the states were interested, be carried into execution by that department of the general government in which they were all to be represented — the congress of the United States?

Later he asserted that the doctrine of federal exclusivity "removes those causes which have contributed more than any other to disturb that harmony which is essential to the continuance of the Union." Wayne concluded by observing, "If there are not now agencies enough to make the assertion of the right to fugitives convenient to their owners, congress can multiply them. But if it should not be done, better is it that the inconvenience should be borne than that the states should be brought into collision upon this subject, as they have been."

At the same time, Wayne was committed to the view that slavery had a special significance in the constitutional order. Both aspects of his jurisprudence were on display in the 1849 decision in *The Passenger Cases*. In that instance he voted to strike down state laws that imposed taxes on immigrants as inconsistent with the grant of power to Congress by the commerce clause. At the same time, addressing the possibility that Congress might constitutionally require the Southern states to accept the immigration of free blacks, Wayne asserted that

all the political sovereignty of the United States, within the States, must be exercised . . . according to what was the actual condition of the States in their domestic institutions when the Constitution was formed, until a State shall please to alter them. The Constitution was formed by States in which slavery existed, and was not likely to be relinquished, and States in which slavery had been, but was abolished, or for the prospective abolition of which provision had been made by law. The undisturbed continuance of that difference between the States at that time, unless it might be changed by a State itself, was the recognized condition in the Constitution for the national Union. It has that, and can have no other foundation.

After citing the slave trade clause and "other clauses" to support this view, Wayne continued:

That it is a very narrow view of the Constitution which supposes that any political sovereign right given by it can be exercised, or was meant to be used, by the United States in such a way as to dissolve, or even disquiet, the fundamental organization of either of the States. The Constitution is to be interpreted by what was the condition of the parties to it when it was formed, by their object and purpose in forming it, and by the actual recognition in it of the dissimilar institutions of the States. The exercise of constitutional power by the United States, or the consequence of its exercise, are not to be concluded by the summary logic of ifs and syllogisms.

In *Prigg*, Wayne's proslavery constitutionalism had been moderated by his commitment to national unity. On the issue of slavery in the territories, the same commitment may have had precisely the opposite effect. By 1856 the principle of geographical division that had underlain the Missouri Compromise was clearly dead, and it had become clear to many observers that continued reliance on the doctrine of popular sovereignty could lead only to ongoing sectional strife as proslavery and antislavery forces contended for control of the government of individual territories. The only alternatives were a firm commitment to a principle that would either outlaw or allow slavery in all of the territories. Wayne would seize on *Dred Scott* as a vehicle to constitutionalize the latter principle.

In many ways, John Catron of Tennessee was the epitome of the moderate Southern Democrat in 1856. The details of Catron's early life are less well established than those of other members of the Taney Court, but it appears that he was born into the Kettering family of western Pennsylvania in 1781. During his childhood Catron's family moved first to western Virginia and then to Kentucky. In both areas Catron lived on farms and acquired his formal education in local common schools. Subsequently, Catron changed his name and moved to Tennessee, beginning to read law in April 1812 and being admitted to the bar in late 1815. He inherited a practice from a local attorney who was elected to Congress; later Catron was appointed by the legislature to be the local prosecutor.

In 1818 Catron moved to Nashville, where he became known for his expertise in issues involving title to real property. Such issues were particularly important and complex in Tennessee, and Catron was therefore a logical choice to fill a vacancy on the state supreme court in 1824. He remained on that court until 1835, serving the last six years as chief justice.

Catron's 1834 opinion in *Fisher's Negroes v. Dabbs* clearly revealed his attitude toward slavery. In concluding that a manumission clause in a will was valid only if the freed slaves were sent to Liberia, Catron declared that "the slave, who receives the protection and care of a tolerable master, holds a condition here, superior to the negro who is freed from domestic slavery. . . . The freed black man lives amongst us without motive and without hope." He also declared that "nothing can be more untrue than that the free negro is more respectable as a member of society in the nonslaveholding than in the slaveholding States. In each, he is a degraded outcast, and his fancied freedom a delusion. . . . Generally, and almost universally, society suffers, and the negro suffers by manumission."

Catron had served under Andrew Jackson in the army and was an early and ardent supporter of Jackson's presidential ambitions. Catron supported not only Jackson himself but also the aspirations of Martin Van Buren, Jackson's anointed successor. Catron's support of Van Buren put him at odds with a number of important state political leaders in Tennessee, and when the state supreme court was reconstituted in 1836, Catron lost his position. After leaving the bench, he campaigned vigorously for Van Buren in the election of 1836. Subsequently, Catron was amply rewarded for his loyalty. In the waning days of the Jackson administration, Tennessee was removed from the Sixth Circuit and placed in a new circuit with Kentucky and Missouri. At the same time, a new position on the Supreme Court was created. Catron was immediately appointed by Jackson to fill the new seat, and Van Buren reaffirmed the appointment after succeeding to the presidency. The Senate quickly confirmed Catron, and he took his seat on March 8, 1837.

Catron showed a clear willingness to compromise on slavery-related issues in *Prigg*, in which he joined Story's majority opinion without comment. Moreover, for most of his life Catron's views on the territorial issue were those of a moderate nationalist Democrat. In 1848 he privately advocated the extension of the Missouri Compromise line to the Pacific and declared that if he were a member of Congress, he would vote to exclude slavery from Oregon. Catron no doubt viewed this approach as a means to permanently resolve the territorial issue on a relatively amicable basis, much as the supporters of the Missouri Compromise had believed that they had found a means to remove the irritant of the territorial issue from national politics. However, these views would change in the wake of the political turmoil of the mid-1850s.

Whereas the Southerners on the *Dred Scott* Court would ultimately prove to be united on the issue of slavery in the territories, their Northern counterparts would be deeply divided. In 1856 the views of the Northern justices on slavery-related issues reflected a cross-section of Northern opinion more generally. Northern Democrats were united in their opposition to those to whom they referred as "Black Republicans" and remained committed to cooperation with the dominant Southern wing of their party. Republicans, by contrast, were openly committed to the principle of sectional struggle. Finally, a substantial number of former Whigs found the doctrines of both major parties distasteful; when the Know Nothing Party collapsed after the election of 1856, this faction had no comfortable affiliation. The perspectives of each of these groups were clearly represented on the Court that considered *Dred Scott*.

Robert C. Grier was born on March 5, 1794, in Cumberland County, Pennsylvania. The son of a Presbyterian minister and schoolmaster, Grier received a thorough classical education at home before being admitted to Dickinson College in 1811 and graduating the following year. Grier then returned home to Northumberland to assist his father in operating a school there, assuming full responsibility for the school after his father's death in 1815. After studying law in his spare time, Grier was admitted to the local bar in 1817.

Grier soon moved to the Pittsburgh area, where he became active in politics. Initially, he espoused the Federalist cause, but he soon converted to the Democratic Party and actively supported Andrew Jackson in his presidential campaigns. In 1833 Grier became president judge of the district court of Allegheny County, where he became known for assertive jury charges that at times resembled the words of an advocate more than those of an impartial judge.

Grier's distaste for abolitionists was well known. On one occasion, when a letter announcing an abolitionist meeting was read in the Presbyterian church in which Grier was an elder, he rose and objected, condemning the abolitionist cause as unconstitutional and seditious and declaring that it should be rejected by all good Christians and loyal citizens. These views stood Grier in good stead when Polk was considering a replacement for Justice Henry Baldwin of Pennsylvania, whose seat had been vacant since Baldwin had died in office on April 21, 1844. Four congressmen from the adjoining slave state of Maryland urged Polk to select Grier and identified him as one who "acknowledges the right of the master to his slave and will enforce it irrespective of the clogs from time to time attempted to be thrown around it by state legislation." Polk sent Grier's nomination to the Senate on August 3, 1846, and the nomination was approved with no apparent opposition the next day.

Prior to *Dred Scott*, Grier's solicitude for what he viewed as the legitimate rights of slaveowners was apparent in a number of the decisions he made while sitting on circuit. For example, in *United States v. Hanaway*, his charge to the jury had reiterated the standard claim that Northern acceptance of the fugitive slave clause was the price for Southern acquiescence in the Constitution, asserting that "if individuals or state legislatures in the North can succeed in thwarting and obstructing the execution of this article of our confederation, and the rights guaranteed to the South thereby, they have no right to complain if the people of the South shall treat the constitution as virtually annulled by the consent of the North and seek secession from any alliance with open and avowed covenant breakers."

In 1852 a similar worldview informed Grier's approach to *Oliver v. Kauffman*, which involved issues that were in some ways similar to those the Court would consider in *Dred Scott* itself. In form, *Kauffman* was an action by a slaveowner to recover damages against several Pennsylvania residents who had allegedly harbored fugitives who had escaped from the plaintiff in Maryland. In 1847, prior to their escape, the fugitives had been taken through Pennsylvania in transit from Arkansas to Maryland. Among other things, the defendants argued that the slaves had become free by virtue of Pennsylvania law when they had passed through the state, that they had retained their freedom even after they had reached Maryland, and that therefore they had not been fugitive slaves at the time of their escape.

Grier began his charge to the jury by warning that "no theories or opinion which you or we may entertain with regard to liberty or human rights, or the policy or justice of a system of domestic slavery, can have a place on the bench or in the jury box." He then held that the escapees had been slaves as a matter of law at the time that they had fled from Maryland. He conceded that in *Somerset*, "Lord Mansfield has said some pretty things . . . which are often quoted as principles of common law" but characterized Mansfield's antislavery language as "rhetorical flourishes rather than legal dogmas." Relying with obvious approval on the Supreme Court's recent decision in *Strader v. Graham*, Grier concluded that the status of the fugitives at the time they had escaped was determined by the law of Maryland, and that under Maryland law they had been slaves. Given his position in *Kauffman*, Grier was unlikely to be sympathetic to the arguments of Dred Scott.

Samuel Nelson of New York was no more favorably disposed to the antislavery forces. Nelson filled the seat that had been vacated by the death of Smith Thompson in December 1843. The effort to replace Thompson had been handicapped by the complex political situation of the early 1840s. The presidency at that time was held by John Tyler, who by that time had thoroughly alienated the Whigs under whose banner he had been elected vice president. Tyler's difficulties in filling Thompson's seat reflected the awkwardness of his political position. After considering the possibility of nominating Democrat Martin Van Buren to replace Thompson, Tyler initially nominated John C. Spencer, a New York Whig from his own cabinet. Spencer was a man of great intellectual ability; however, he had alienated orthodox Whigs by continuing to serve under Tyler after Tyler's break with the party. Faced with opposition from the members of Spencer's own party, the nomination was rejected by the Senate. Tyler then selected Reuben H. Walworth, the chancellor of New York. If confirmed, Walworth might well have added a strong antislavery voice to the Court. Prior to the *Prigg* decision, in *Jack v. Martin* he had expressed the view that Congress lacked the authority to pass legislation to enforce the fugitive slave clause. Although the Senate also failed to confirm Walworth, his defeat seems to have been based not on slavery-related issues but rather on his personal unpopularity and the fear that he would be replaced in New York by a Democrat. Finally, in February 1845, Tyler — now a lame duck — turned to Democrat Samuel Nelson, the chief justice of the New York Supreme Court. Nelson was quickly confirmed and took his seat on February 13.

Samuel Nelson was born in 1792 in Hebron, New York. Initially planning to become a minister, he attended Middlebury College, graduating in 1813. Turning to law, he studied in the offices of Savage and Woods in Salem, New York, and then with Judge Woods after he moved to Madison. Nelson was admitted to the bar in 1817, entered politics, and served as a postmaster for three years before being appointed a judge of the Sixth Circuit in New York in 1823. In 1831 he was elevated to the state supreme court as an associate justice, eventually becoming chief justice of the court in 1837.

Even before he came to the Supreme Court, Nelson had produced at least one notable opinion on the constitutional issues related to slavery. Like Walworth, Nelson had been called upon to interpret the fugitive slave clause in *Jack v. Martin*. However, unlike Walworth, Nelson had adopted the position that ultimately prevailed in *Prigg*, concluding that Congress possessed authority to adopt legislation enforcing the constitutional rights of claimants. Once he was on the Court, his circuit opinions were notable for an apparent lack of zeal in enforcing the federal prohibition on the slave trade. Thus, Nelson was also an unlikely ally for Dred Scott.

John McLean stood at the other end of the political spectrum from Nelson and Grier and his Southern brethren on the issue of slavery in the territories. McLean was born in northern New Jersey on May 8, 1787. During his early years, McLean's family moved steadily westward, journeying first to Morgantown, Virginia, and later to the vicinity of Lexington, Kentucky, before finally settling in Warren County, Ohio, in 1798. There McLean received his first formal education in a neighborhood school. He later continued his studies in Cincinnati. Beginning in 1804, McLean served two years as an apprentice to the clerk of the local court of common pleas. During this period he also studied law with Arthur St. Clair Jr., the son of the territorial governor. McLean purchased a printing office in 1806 and in 1807 began publishing the Lebanon *Western Star*. The same year, he married Rebecca Edwards. In 1810 McLean disposed of the newspaper and turned to the practice of law as his profession.

Prior to his appointment to the Supreme Court, McLean held a variety of different government positions. He served in the House of Representatives from 1812 to 1816, was a member of the Ohio Supreme Court from 1816 to 1823, and was postmaster general under both James Monroe and John Quincy Adams from 1823 to 1829. In 1829 McLean became Andrew Jackson's first appointment to the Court. He was confirmed without incident and replaced Robert Trimble on March 7, 1829.

During his long tenure on the Court, McLean was a staunch nationalist, in general arguing for a broad view of federal power and a limited conception of state power to act concurrently in matters over which the federal government had constitutional authority. McLean was also a committed opponent of slavery. For example, while sitting on the Ohio Supreme Court in 1817, he had declared in dictum that "viewing the question abstractly I could not hesitate to declare that a slave in any state or country, according to the immutable principles of natural justice, is entitled to his freedom; that, that which had its origin in usurpation and fraud can never be sanctified into a right."

Taken alone, this language might be seen as supporting the observations of Thomas Hart Benton, who once declared that McLean was "abolitionist enough for any body outside of a mad house — & his wife is abolitionist enough for all those who ought to be in one." McLean's constitutional jurisprudence was in fact clearly influenced by his views on slavery. Nonetheless, he was by no means the antislavery zealot portrayed by Benton.

The limits of McLean's commitment to the antislavery cause were apparent in his approach to the issue of fugitive slaves. To be sure, in *Prigg v. Pennsylvania* he was the only justice to take a more antislavery position than Justice Story, arguing alone that states should be allowed to impose procedures that restricted the slaveowner's right of recaption. At the same time, McLean did not fully embrace the radical antislavery position. He rejected the assault on the constitutionality of the Fugitive Slave Act of 1793, thereby upholding congressional authority to adopt legislation implementing the fugitive slave clause.

In *Dred Scott* McLean would be influenced not only by his jurisprudential philosophy and views on slavery but also by the exigencies of his lifelong pursuit of the presidency. As early as 1832 he had flirted with the idea of running as the candidate of the Anti-Masonic Party. However, prior to the political realignment of the early 1850s, he became closely associated with the Whigs and was a major factor in the early maneuvering for the Whig nomination for the election of 1848. During that campaign, McLean began with strong support among Northern Whigs. Thus, one of his primary goals was to draw Southern party members to his banner. In making his case for the nomination, McLean presented himself as a non-ideological reform candidate, juxtaposing his candidacy with that of professional politicians such as Clay and Webster. The emergence of the Wilmot Proviso as a major national issue played a significant role in undermining this strategy. Once the question of slavery in the territories assumed such prominence, Southern Whigs were unlikely to support a person such as McLean, whose antislavery credentials were already well established.

After it became clear that he would not become the Whig candidate, many prominent adherents to the free-soil movement sought to enlist McLean as the candidate of the Free Soil Party. With the Wilmot Proviso being the primary focus of the dispute over slavery in the late 1840s, even radical free soilers saw McLean's views as entirely consistent with free-soil doctrine. However, understanding that the Free Soil candidate had no real chance to win the election in 1848, McLean demurred. He hoped to make another strong run for the Whig nomination in 1852 and believed that running on the Free Soil ticket in 1848 would undermine such a campaign.

Despite his ambitions, McLean never emerged as a serious contender for the nomination in 1852. By 1856 the American political landscape had changed dramatically. The Whig Party had disintegrated, and both the nativist Know Nothings and the antislavery Republicans were seeking to fill the resulting vacuum and emerge as the primary opposition to the Democrats. McLean first courted the Know Nothings, characterizing nativism as a much-needed reform movement. When Millard Fillmore was nominated as the Know Nothing candidate in February 1856, McLean and his supporters turned to the Republican Party as the vehicle to advance his presidential ambitions. He and John Fremont soon emerged as the primary contenders for the 1856 Republican nomination.

The tactical problem that confronted McLean and his supporters in 1856 was quite different from that which they had faced in his pursuit of the Whig nomination in 1848. Rather than appealing to Southerners, McLean's task in 1856 was to convince some elements of the Republican Party that his antislavery views were sufficiently radical to merit their support. A number of McLean's opponents asserted (with

{ *Chapter 6* }

some justification) that his embrace of Republicanism was as much a matter of convenience as conviction. For example, Republican Sen. Benjamin F. Wade privately complained that "if he is with us at all it is but timidly and feebly." Radicals — whose distaste for the Fugitive Slave Laws of 1793 and 1850 was often as intense as their opposition to the expansion of slavery into the territories — were particularly disturbed by McLean's conclusion that Congress did in fact have authority to adopt legislation enforcing the fugitive slave clause. Thus, McLean's consistent willingness to enforce the provisions of the federal statutes led one Ohio Republican to assert that McLean "has *no sentiment* or *sympathy* with the *principle of universal Liberty.*"

Prior to 1856, some Republicans were also dissatisfied with McLean's position on the Kansas-Nebraska Act and its aftermath. In 1847 he had propounded a view that in essence turned the Southern theory of nonintervention on its head. His argument began with the basic premise of *Somerset*, which held that slavery could not legally exist in the absence of positive law recognizing the relationship. McLean then contended that Congress lacked the constitutional power to establish slavery in the territories held by the federal government. Therefore, under this theory, slaves could not be held in those territories prior to statehood.

Some Republicans objected that this theory did not establish the power of Congress to pass legislation affirmatively prohibiting slavery in the territories. Indeed, the argument might be taken to imply that Congress lacked such authority, thereby undercutting the contention that Southerners had broken a solemn pledge when they engineered the repeal of the Missouri Compromise. McLean's Republican critics also faulted him for his failure to condemn the tactics employed by the proslavery forces in Kansas. Seeking to blunt these objections, his supporters urged McLean to denounce the repeal in the strongest terms. *Dred Scott* would present him with the opportunity to make a political statement that would appeal to the more radical elements of the Republican Party. But whether or not McLean took that opportunity, he remained the strongest antislavery voice on the Taney Court.

Benjamin Robbins Curtis was cut from quite different cloth. Curtis was born on November 4, 1809, in Watertown, Massachusetts. He was educated at Harvard University and Harvard Law School, where he studied under Joseph Story. After briefly practicing in Northfield,

Massachusetts, where he was admitted to the bar in September 1834, Curtis associated himself with Charles Pelham Curtis, a distant relative who had an established practice in Boston. Except for his interlude on the Supreme Court, Curtis remained in private practice in Boston until his death.

Like orthodox Massachusetts Whigs generally, Curtis believed that slavery was wrong. However, for Curtis — like other conservative Whigs such as Daniel Webster — opposition to slavery was always subordinate to his concern for the maintenance of an appropriate relationship between the states of the Union. Curtis's private correspondence reflects his understanding that disputes over slavery represented a clear threat to this relationship. His awareness of this threat is also demonstrated in his advocacy of a set of closely related legal and political doctrines designed to ease tensions between free states and slave states. In the legal context, Curtis argued that issues of slavery should not be treated differently than other questions of status. Politically, he contended that the Northern states should recognize the importance of slavery to the interests of the South and give those interests substantial consideration in slavery-related policy decisions.

As early as 1836, Curtis showed a willingness to defend what he saw as the legitimate interests of slaveowners, arguing unsuccessfully in *Commonwealth v. Aves* that, under state law, a Louisiana slaveowner should retain dominion over a slave voluntarily brought into Massachusetts on a temporary sojourn. However, prior to his appointment to the Court, Curtis's most important public pronouncement on slavery came in a November 1850 speech counseling obedience to the newly strengthened Fugitive Slave Act. The speech argued that the state of Massachusetts and its citizens were bound to respect the act by virtue of the state's decision to accept the constitutional compact, which included the fugitive slave clause. In addition, Curtis made two points that, taken together, summarized his general position on the issues of fugitive slaves. First, he contended that Massachusetts owed no obligation to escaped slaves: "With the rights of [fugitive slaves] I firmly believe Massachusetts has nothing to do. It is enough for us that they have no right to be *here*. Our peace and safety they have no right to invade; whether they come as fugitives, and being here, act as rebels against our law, or whether they come as armed invaders.

Whatever natural rights they have, and I admit those natural rights to their fullest extent, *this* is not the *soil* on which to vindicate them."

In addition, Curtis emphasized the need to seek accommodation with the slave states — a need that he viewed as deriving as much from geography as the existence of the Union:

> Without an obligation to restore fugitives from service, Constitution or no Constitution, we could not expect to live in peace with the slave-holding states. . . . You may break up the Constitution and the Union to-morrow . . . you may do it in any conceivable or inconceivable way; you may draw the geographical line between slave-holding and nonslave-holding *anywhere;* but when we have settled down, they will have their institutions and we shall have ours. One is as much a fact as the other. One engages the interests and feelings and passions of men as much as the other. And how long can we live in peace, side by side, without some provision by compact, to meet this case? Not one year.

This speech clearly reflected the importance of living in harmony with the slave states as a dominant theme in Curtis's thinking. Not surprisingly, when the local federal marshals sought a formal legal opinion vindicating the constitutionality of the Fugitive Slave Act, Curtis was the man they asked to produce the opinion.

His rejection of radical antislavery doctrine served Curtis well when Levi Woodbury died on March 4, 1851, creating a vacancy on the Supreme Court. By custom, Woodbury was to be replaced by a New Englander. President Millard Fillmore sought a person who would "combine a vigorous constitution with high moral and intellectual qualifications, a good judicial mind, and such age as gives a prospect of long service." Moreover, as a strong supporter of the Compromise of 1850, Fillmore was unlikely to choose a nominee from the radical antislavery wing of his party. The forty-two-year-old Curtis thus became a logical choice. With the strong endorsement of Daniel Webster, Curtis was given a recess appointment on September 22, 1851, and was subsequently confirmed by the Senate over the objections of the radical antislavery forces.

The political upheaval of the mid-1850s left Curtis a man without a party. As a supporter of the Compromise of 1850, he could have no love for a Republican Party that focused on the issue of slavery and derided the Southern states. At the same time, unlike (for example) Nelson and Grier, Curtis was not politically aligned with the governing elites of the South. Thus, of all the members of the Court in 1856, Curtis was perhaps the best positioned to make a dispassionate analysis of the legal issues that would be presented to the Court in *Dred Scott*. Given the situation in the mid-1850s, however, even Curtis could not fail to take into account the potential ramifications of the case for the sectional conflict. Indeed, it was politics more than law that would ultimately dictate the approaches of the various justices to many of the issues presented by the case.

CHAPTER 7

Arguments and Deliberations

By the time the *Dred Scott* case was argued before the Supreme Court, both sides had obtained volunteer assistance from attorneys with prominent national reputations. On October 14, 1854, Hugh Garland died. He was replaced as counsel for Sanford by Reverdy Johnson of Maryland and Henry S. Geyer of Missouri. Johnson, a former U.S. senator who had served as attorney general under Zachary Taylor, was generally recognized as one of the leading constitutional lawyers in the country. Geyer had served as a senator from Missouri and was regarded as perhaps the greatest lawyer in the state.

Geyer and Johnson were opposed by Montgomery Blair of Maryland. Blair was an apt choice to represent the Scotts in the Supreme Court. Born in Kentucky in 1813, Blair was a former slaveowner whose personal odyssey epitomized the impact of disputes over slavery on the structure of American politics more generally. His father, Frances Preston Blair, was a member of Andrew Jackson's "kitchen cabinet," and, after moving to Saint Louis in 1836, Montgomery had become a protégé of Thomas Hart Benton. In the wake of the bitter dispute over the Wilmot Proviso, Blair temporarily abandoned the Democratic Party in 1848, supporting Free Soil candidate Martin Van Buren in preference to Lewis Cass, the Democratic nominee. Soon thereafter, Blair returned to the Democratic fold and campaigned enthusiastically in support of Franklin Pierce for president in 1852. Blair moved to Washington, D.C., in 1853, and in early 1855, Pierce selected him to be the solicitor for the newly created Court of Claims. Nonetheless, by 1856 the escalating conflict in Kansas had once again alienated Blair from the dominant faction in the Democratic Party and led him to join the newly formed Republican Party. He would later serve as postmaster general under Abraham Lincoln.

Field had written to Blair requesting his aid as early as May 24,

1854. After Field repeated his request on December 24, emphasizing the importance of the principles involved in the case, Blair agreed to represent Dred Scott, without payment, on December 30 — the same day that Field filed his appeal with the Supreme Court. Blair in turn persuaded Gamaliel Bailey, the editor of the abolitionist newspaper *National Era*, to raise the funds necessary to cover court costs and incidental expenses.

The Court itself did not finally reach the *Dred Scott* case until February 1856. On February 7, Montgomery Blair filed the only written brief of which there is any surviving record. In his attack on the lower-court decision, Blair did not advert directly to *Strader v. Graham*. Nor did the brief make any mention of the time Scott had spent at Fort Snelling. Instead, Blair focused solely on Scott's residence in Illinois as the basis for the claim that he should be declared a free man. Blair rejected the claim that the Illinois prohibition on slavery should be viewed as a penal law, and also the view that Scott's status as a slave had simply been suspended while he lived in Illinois. Rather, Blair argued that by voluntarily bringing Scott to live for an extended period in Illinois with the knowledge that slavery was forbidden there, Emerson had in effect voluntarily emancipated Scott, and that, prior to the decision in *Scott v. Emerson*, the Missouri courts had consistently recognized such emancipations as final. Scott, Blair argued, was entitled to the benefit of these pre-*Emerson* rules, which, he noted, were consistent with the principles that had been adopted by a variety of other slave states.

From the perspective of modern commentators such as Don E. Fehrenbacher and Paul Finkelman, Blair's decision to rely solely on Dred Scott's time in Illinois seems almost inexplicable. Finkelman, for example, argues that Blair could have relied on Scott's journey to Fort Snelling to distinguish *Strader*. The Court in *Strader* had held only that Kentucky was not bound to respect the freedom that had been granted to erstwhile slaves by the law of another state — Ohio. During his time at Fort Snelling, Scott had become free by virtue of a *federal* statute — the Northwest Ordinance. Finkelman asserts that, in this context, Blair should have argued that Missouri was bound by the supremacy clause to vindicate Scott's freedom upon his return to that state.

However, the idea that the Northwest Ordinance would have a more expansive extraterritorial effect than the law of Illinois seems to have been inconceivable to Blair. Indeed, no one appears to have made such a claim at any stage of the case. If the status of only Dred Scott himself had been at issue, the tactical decision to ignore the time spent at Fort Snelling would have been entirely plausible. Given the makeup of the Court and its recent decision in *Strader*, Blair faced an uphill struggle in any event, particularly with respect to the Southern members of the Court. Adverting to the politically explosive issue of the status of the Missouri Compromise would have created the danger of alienating these justices. Moreover, it would have added nothing to the strength of his case. If the courts of Missouri were entitled to disregard the Illinois prohibition on slavery, then they had no greater obligation to recognize Scott's freedom based on his residence in the Wisconsin Territory. Indeed, as Field observed in a letter to Blair, the argument based on Scott's time in Illinois was actually stronger than that founded on his time in the Wisconsin Territory. Whereas the Missouri Compromise simply provided that slavery "shall be and is . . . forever prohibited" north of 36 degrees, 30 minutes, the Illinois state constitution explicitly stated that the introduction of a slave into the state would result in the emancipation of the slave. In short, the discussion of the Missouri Compromise may well have appeared to carry substantial risks with little hope of a corresponding reward.

However, when Harriet and Eliza are considered in the equation, the glaring flaw in Blair's strategy emerges clearly. Neither had ever lived in the state of Illinois. The antislavery provisions of the Missouri Compromise provided the *only* basis on which they could claim their freedom. It seems highly unlikely that Blair made a conscious decision to sacrifice Dred Scott's wife and daughter for a tactical advantage; the most plausible explanation for his strategy is that he simply did not focus on the difference between the relative legal positions of Dred Scott and the other members of the Scott family.

In any event, the majority of the brief focused not on the issue of Scott's freedom but instead on a defense of the lower court's conclusion that he could be considered a citizen of Missouri for the purpose of diversity jurisdiction. One conceivable explanation for this rather curious strategy is that Blair might have been seeking to preempt an anticipated attack on the lower-court ruling by Sanford's attorneys. But if this was Blair's motivation, his execution was singularly inept. His argument dealt only with the *substance* of the claim that the lower court had jurisdiction over the case as an initial matter, tracking the argument of Judge Wells and citing a number of lower-court decisions that had allowed free African Americans to participate in diversity actions both as plaintiffs and defendants. Blair failed to even mention the possibility that the jurisdiction issue was not properly before the Supreme Court at all — an argument that, as we will see, had considerable force and even turned out to be persuasive to a number of the justices.

Alternatively, Blair may have been influenced by a letter from Roswell Field suggesting that a favorable ruling by the Supreme Court on the substance of the jurisdiction question could have important collateral benefits. Field believed that if free African Americans were deemed to be citizens for purposes of diversity jurisdiction, then a putative slave seized and held under the provisions of the Fugitive Slave Act of 1850 could obtain a jury trial in the state where he had been captured by the simple expedient of instituting a suit for freedom in federal court against the person who claimed him. Jurisdiction for such a lawsuit would be based on the theory that the African American who had been seized was a citizen of the state where he had been found.

If vindicating this position was in fact Blair's motivation for failing to advert to the procedural bar against consideration of the jurisdiction issue, then he was guilty of sacrificing the interests of his client in order to make a speculative attempt to advance the goals of the broader antislavery movement. Moreover, although some modern commentators have accepted Field's argument at face value, the success of this strategy would in fact have been far from certain even if free African Americans had been held to be citizens for purposes of diversity jurisdiction. Apparently, Field mistakenly believed that the federal courts were required by the Constitution to take jurisdiction over cases based upon diversity of citizenship. In fact, in order to bring an action in federal court, one must satisfy not only the relevant constitutional minima but also the statutory requirements imposed by Congress. Courts would probably have held that the general diversity jurisdiction established by statute could not be used to circumvent the more specific provisions of the subsequently adopted Fugitive Slave Act of 1850. Under this view, an alleged escapee might file his suit for freedom in federal court, but only in the state where his master resided, *after* the putative escapee had been returned to that state. Nonetheless, Field clearly believed that a favorable ruling on the merits of the citizenship issue would benefit fugitive slaves, and a similar belief may have informed Blair's tactics.

In seeking to vindicate the lower court's ruling on African American citizenship, Blair observed that in many cases prior to *Dred Scott*, federal courts had recognized free African Americans for purposes of diversity jurisdiction without even discussing the issue. He conceded that "there is a recognised social distinction which excludes [African Americans] from association with whites on equal terms in all the States" and that in many states free blacks were denied political rights. Blair contended, however, that citizenship was not premised on the possession of these rights, but that any person who was "a freeman . . . not a foreigner, not a slave" should be considered a citizen for constitutional purposes. He also observed that, although Congress had generally limited naturalization to free whites, specific treaties had granted American citizenship to members of a number of Indian tribes and to the inhabitants of Louisiana and California without regard to race.

Against the background of these written arguments, *Dred Scott* was first argued before the Supreme Court on February 11, 12, 13, and 14. While each attorney was normally allowed two hours to make his argument, on the motion of Reverdy Johnson, the Court extended the allotted time to three hours. The newspaper reports of the arguments were very brief, but one point emerges clearly. Whether gratuitously or because of the situation of Harriet and Eliza, Johnson and Geyer contended that Congress lacked the authority to prohibit slavery in the territories acquired from France in the Louisiana Purchase. This marked the first time such an argument was made during the litigation over the status of Dred Scott and his family.

The introduction of this argument fundamentally changed the nature of the *Dred Scott* litigation. By challenging the constitutionality of the Missouri Compromise, Johnson and Geyer were doing nothing less than inviting the Court to involve itself directly in the political crisis that was deeply dividing the country. Not surprisingly, for the first time, the popular press began to take notice of the case. For example, on February 15 Horace Greeley reported in the *New York Daily Tribune* that the Supreme Court would soon decide "a most important case, involving the validity (in its day) of the Missouri restriction."

Nonetheless, public discussions of *Dred Scott* at this point were far less numerous and prominent than newspaper accounts of other aspects of the sectional conflict, including cases such as In re *Booth and Rycraft* from Wisconsin and *Lemmon v. The People* from New York.

In hindsight, the relative lack of attention paid to *Dred Scott* in early 1856 seems almost perverse. Yet, from the perspective of most observers at that time, one can easily see how the *Booth* and *Lemmon* cases might have seemed of greater significance. *Booth* arose from the efforts of the state of Wisconsin to nullify the Fugitive Slave Act of 1850, and in *Lemmon* a New York court had freed the slaves of a Virginia resident who was doing nothing more than passing through New York in transit to Texas. In each case, the relationship between the facts of the situation and the sectional conflict was direct and apparent. By contrast, *Dred Scott* appeared to involve nothing more than the efforts of a Missouri court to determine the status of an African American who was in Missouri and was a resident of that state. The sectional implications of the case emerged only indirectly and required more explanation. Moreover, prior to the arguments of February 1856, none of the courts that had dealt with the case had discussed the constitutionality of the Missouri Compromise, and even after the issue had been raised in the arguments of Geyer and Johnson, it was far from clear that the Supreme Court would reach that question. Indeed, the decision to discuss the Missouri Compromise came only after a complex series of deliberations that reflected the interaction of nine justices with widely differing views on both the morality of slavery generally and its relationship to the sectional conflict more specifically.

The Court discussed *Dred Scott* in conference a number of times between the completion of the oral arguments and May 12. In an account that seems to be confirmed by the private correspondence, James Harvey, a confidant of Justice John McLean, reported in the *New York Daily Tribune* that the Southern justices planned to decide the case on narrow grounds, avoiding a discussion of the Missouri Compromise altogether, but that McLean and perhaps other Northern justices would vindicate the constitutionality of the compromise in dissent. Similarly, in a letter to his uncle George Ticknor on April 8, Justice Benjamin Robbins Curtis wrote that "the court will not decide the question of the Missouri Compromise line — a majority of the judges being of opinion that it is not necessary to do so."

At the same time, the justices were deeply divided over a technical issue — the question of whether the issue of Dred Scott's citizenship was properly before the Court. In 1856 state courts generally would have held that the defendant had clearly waived all objections to jurisdiction by defending on the merits. However, some of the justices believed that, because the subject-matter jurisdiction of the federal courts was limited by the terms of the Constitution itself, a different rule should apply in cases in which a challenge to diversity of citizenship was raised. Under these circumstances, a bisectional coalition including Chief Justice Taney of Maryland and Justices Wayne of Georgia, Daniel of Virginia, and Curtis of Massachusetts insisted that the Court could properly review the record to determine whether the federal courts had jurisdiction over the case. Conversely, an equally bisectional group composed of Justices McLean of Ohio, Catron of Tennessee, Grier of Pennsylvania, and Campbell of Alabama insisted that the standard rule of waiver was applicable. The balance of power on the issue was held by Justice Nelson of New York. While Nelson was inclined to agree with the Taney group, he remained uncertain. To allow Nelson to resolve his uncertainty, the justices agreed unanimously to have the case reargued, and on May 12 the Court issued the requisite order. The attorneys were directed to give special attention to the questions of whether the plea in abatement was properly before the Court and, if the decision on jurisdiction was reviewable, whether Dred Scott could be considered a citizen for purposes of diversity jurisdiction.

Some Republican newspapers immediately condemned the decision, asserting that the postponement was motivated by the desire of the Southern and Democratic justices to prevent McLean and Curtis from issuing opinions supporting the constitutionality of the Missouri Compromise during the presidential campaign. For example, a columnist for the *New York Daily Tribune* declared that "the black gowns have come to be artful dodgers. The minority were prepared to meet the issue [of slavery in the territories] broadly and distinctly; but the controlling members were not quite ready . . . to open the opportunity for a demolition of the fraudulent pretenses that have been set up in Congress on this question." Prominent Republicans would later repeat this charge. The evidence suggests that at least some of the justices were indeed reluctant to inject a controversial ruling on slavery directly into the campaign. However, the unanimity of the decision to postpone negates any implication that the postponement was driven by partisan or sectional considerations. In any event, at the time the reargument was ordered, the interest in the case shown by the *New York Daily Tribune* was still the exception rather than the rule. Most newspapers had no reaction to the order at all.

In the interim between the issuance of the order and the reargument in December 1856, a number of factors intervened to change the dynamic of *Dred Scott*. The first significant development was jurisprudential. Only two days after the order for reargument, the Court handed down its decision in *Pease v. Peck*. On its face, *Pease* was entirely unrelated to the dispute over slavery in the territories. Instead, the case (which had begun as a diversity action) revolved around a highly technical issue of Michigan statutory law. All members of the Court conceded that even under the regime of *Swift v. Tyson*, the case should be governed by Michigan law. The problem was that the most recent interpretation of Michigan law by the state supreme court was apparently inconsistent with prior decisions from the same court. Over the dissents of Justices Campbell and Daniel, Justice Grier concluded for the Court that, under those circumstances, the Supreme Court was not bound to follow the most recent rule laid down by the state supreme court but was instead free to make an independent judgment on the proper rule to be applied.

George Ticknor Curtis, a prominent Massachusetts attorney who was the brother of Justice Curtis, would later claim that Justice Grier contemporaneously informed a confidant that *Pease* had been decided specifically to release the justices in *Dred Scott* from the obligation to follow the principles laid down by the Missouri Supreme Court in *Scott v. Emerson*. It is difficult to discern the tactical advantage that Grier and the other justices who would later form the *Dred Scott* majority hoped to gain by undermining the authority of the Missouri decision. But whatever motives actually underlay the *Pease* decision, its doctrinal significance was unmistakable. Even if a justice concluded that the nonconstitutional issues in *Dred Scott* should be governed by state law, he could still cite *Pease* and argue that the Scotts should be deemed free under Missouri law.

The political developments between May and December had an even greater impact on the judicial dynamic. During this period the level of sectional tension increased greatly. On May 19 and 20 Sen. Charles Sumner of Massachusetts delivered an intemperate speech in the Senate condemning what he described as "the crime against Kansas." Two days later Sumner was caned on the Senate floor by Rep. Preston Brooks of South Carolina, provoking a furious response from antislavery Northerners. Violence in Kansas worsened, highlighted by such incidents as the attack of proslavery forces in Lawrence, Kansas, and the massacre on Pottawatomie Creek. The election of 1856 was no doubt even more significant. Although Democrat James Buchanan won the presidency in the election of 1856, the strong showing of Republican John Fremont, who carried eleven of sixteen free states, demonstrated the power of the appeal of the combination antislavery, anti-Southern message of the Republicans to large portions of the Northern electorate. In December outgoing President Franklin Pierce added fuel to the fire in his last annual message to Congress, devoting much of the message to a vitriolic attack on the Republican Party, describing the Missouri Compromise as "a mere nullity . . . a monument of error . . . a dead letter in law," and including remarks that suggested to some that he believed existing Supreme Court precedent vindicated the Southern position on the constitutional issues raised by *Dred Scott*. Pierce's message provoked a sharp exchange in Congress over these constitutional issues.

With sectional tensions thus exacerbated, the attorneys made their presentations to the Court in *Dred Scott* in December 1856. Geyer filed a written brief on December 2; Blair followed suit on December 15. Although the case was still not widely discussed in newspapers, its significance had become clear to political insiders. Thus, when Blair opened oral arguments on December 15, he spoke for three hours before a packed courtroom. The next two days were occupied with arguments by Geyer and Johnson. On December 18 the time was divided between Blair and George Ticknor Curtis. The new addition to Scott's legal team was hardly an antislavery zealot; instead, he was a conservative Whig who had supported the Compromise of 1850.

Nonetheless, at the last moment he had agreed to join Blair in the defense of the constitutionality of the restriction on slavery in the Missouri Compromise.

Curtis openly proclaimed his moderate position and took pains to limit his presentation to distinctively legal issues. Given the geographical and political makeup of the Court, Blair would no doubt have been well served by taking a similar approach. However, his presentation is striking for its characterization of the *Dred Scott* case as part of the ongoing struggle between the slave power and the defenders of freedom. Blair asserted:

> The natural division among men wherever born is into those who sympathise with power and dread the people, on one side, and those who dread tyranny and fear the people less, on the other. The power party naturally associates itself with property interests, and institutions which create political privileges. The other naturally allies itself with the advocates of personal rights, and opposes privileges. The contest going on under the issue here presented is but one phase of this ever-continued and ever-varying strife.
>
> Slavery is an institution which vests political power in the few, by the monopoly of the soil, wealth, and knowledge which it creates. This is the most obvious effect on the society or States where it exists, and an obvious consequence is the concentration of power in the hands of those to whom the authority of such societies or States is entrusted in the confederacy of which they form part.
>
> And it is the sense of inequality and privilege which it creates which lies at the bottom of the contest now going on to decide whether new communities of this character shall be created on the unoccupied lands of the confederacy.

Full transcripts of the arguments of Sanford's attorneys were never published. However, reports of the arguments clearly indicate that Geyer and Johnson also took quite different tacks. Geyer emphasized the doctrine of popular sovereignty, connecting it to the values underlying the Revolution. By contrast, Johnson's presentation bristled with Southern indignation against what slaveholders saw as demeaning restrictions on slavery in the territories, condemning "unequal, disparaging and insulting legislation"; characterizing the Missouri Compromise as the "law of the stronger attempted in the exercise of the conqueror's right"; and declaring that "the people of the South do not stand in the relation of servant to the North."

Despite the tenor of these arguments, in theory *Dred Scott* was to be decided on the basis of technical legal doctrine rather than political considerations. In making their arguments, the attorneys were required to address six separate issues.

---

1. Was the issue of Dred Scott's citizenship properly before the Court?

Blair argued that Sanford had waived his right to appeal the jurisdictional issue by pleading to the merits. Geyer and Johnson argued that the defendant did not have the authority to in effect vest the court with jurisdiction by addressing the merits and that the Court therefore was required to dismiss the case if the pleadings on their face did not state facts sufficient to support jurisdiction based on diversity of citizenship.

---

2. Assuming that the Court should address the question, were the Scotts citizens for purposes of the jurisdictional requirements of Article III?

Attorneys for both sides could cite a variety of authorities to support their respective positions. Expanding on the arguments that he had made in 1855, Blair argued first that the term "citizen" generally meant nothing more than "free inhabitant" for federal constitutional purposes; second that the essence of citizenship was not the possession of political rights but rather "the right of protection of life and liberty, to acquire and possess property, and equal taxation"; and finally that even if free blacks were not citizens for purposes of the comity clause, they nonetheless should be considered citizens for purposes of diversity jurisdiction. By contrast, Geyer and Johnson argued that free blacks generally were not citizens and that, in any event, Dred Scott and his family *specifically* were not citizens because (a) as slaves, they were not citizens at birth, and (b) even assuming they were emancipated by Emerson, Emerson had no authority to confer upon them the political status of citizenship.

------

3. Assuming that the Court had jurisdiction over the case, was the Court bound to follow the decision of the Missouri Supreme Court in *Scott v. Emerson*?

Geyer and Johnson argued that this issue was governed by *Strader v. Graham* and that the Court was bound by the decision in *Scott v. Emerson*. Blair, by contrast, correctly observed that *Strader* had decided only that that case had presented no federal question and reiterated his position that, under the rule of *Swift v. Tyson*, the Court should apply the general federal common law in *Dred Scott*, particularly in view of the fact the *Scott v. Emerson* was inconsistent with prior Missouri case law.

------

4. Assuming that the Court was not bound by the decision in *Scott v. Emerson*, had the Scotts established their right to freedom?

On this point Blair delivered a much more sophisticated argument than he had when the case had first been presented to the Court. First, in sharp contrast to his initial brief, Blair carefully distinguished the situation of Dred from those of Harriet and Eliza. Blair continued to rely primarily on Dred's residence in Illinois as the basis for his claim to freedom. At the same time, the argument acknowledged that Harriet's and Eliza's claims could rest only on the antislavery provisions of the Missouri Compromise. Blair also argued that, unlike Dred and Harriet, Eliza had *never* been a slave because she had been born in a jurisdiction where slavery was prohibited by law.

For the first time, Blair sought to exploit a crucial omission from the agreed statement of facts. Even Geyer and Johnson conceded that if Emerson had in fact been domiciled in free territory with the Scotts, then they were entitled to their freedom. Blair pointed out that the statement of facts nowhere explicitly stated that Emerson had been domiciled in Missouri at the time that he had entered military service.

Under those circumstances, Blair argued, the Scotts were entitled to rely on the common-law presumption that a person was domiciled in the jurisdiction in which he lived — in this case, at different times, the state of Illinois and the Wisconsin Territory — and the Scotts were entitled to their freedom for that reason.

Blair also returned to an argument he had made when the case had first been considered. He contended that by voluntarily bringing the Scotts into jurisdictions in which slavery was prohibited by law, Emerson had in effect emancipated the Scotts. Thus, Blair reasoned, the Scotts could not legally have been reenslaved upon their return with Emerson to Missouri. He sought to distinguish *The Slave, Grace* on the ground that, unlike England, slavery was absolutely prohibited by statute in both the state of Illinois and the Wisconsin Territory.

Geyer and Johnson took issue with virtually all of Blair's conclusions. While conceding that Dred Scott at least might have been entitled to his freedom if Emerson had in fact been domiciled in Illinois, Sanford's representatives relied on the general principle that a person who came to a jurisdiction solely because of a military assignment did not become domiciled there. They also denied that the Scotts had been voluntarily emancipated by being brought to reside in free territory, citing a number of authorities for the proposition that Emerson's right to coerce the Scotts had simply been suspended during their common tenure in free territory. Relying heavily on *The Slave, Grace*, Geyer and Johnson concluded that, even leaving constitutional considerations aside, the Scotts were not entitled to their freedom.

————

5. Was the restriction on slavery in the Missouri Compromise constitutional?

In defending the constitutionality of the Missouri Compromise, Blair and Curtis both focused on Article IV, Section 3, paragraph 2 of the Constitution, which states that "Congress shall have power to dispose of and make all needful Rules and Regulations respecting the Territory or other Property belonging to the United States," arguing that this provision armed Congress with plenary authority to govern the territories, including the authority to ban slavery. On one hand, Curtis provided a detailed account of the evolution of this clause at the

Constitutional Convention. Blair, on the other hand, emphasized the long history of Southern acquiescence in such measures and contended that Southerners could not first accept the Missouri Compromise as the price for the admission of Missouri as a slave state and then, thirty years after Missouri had been admitted, repudiate the terms of the bargain by arguing that the restriction on slavery was unconstitutional.

Geyer and Johnson responded by contending that the power granted by Article IV, Section 3, paragraph 2 extended only to the acquisition and disposition of land rather than to determining the rights of the people living on the territory owned by the United States. They conceded that, as an incident to its power to admit new states under Article IV, Section 3, paragraph 1, Congress could institute temporary governments to administer the territories until they had met the prerequisites for statehood. However, Geyer and Johnson contended that, as an implied power, this authority should be interpreted narrowly and did not encompass the prohibition of slavery, which was in no sense necessary for the maintenance of order within the territories. They also relied on the common-property doctrine and characterized Southern acquiescence in previous limitations as expedient compromises in which Southerners had shown a willingness to forgo the enforcement of their rights in the interest of preserving the Union and maintaining sectional harmony.

Unlike the proceedings of the previous February, the December arguments in *Dred Scott* were noted widely in the national press. The quality of Curtis's presentation was almost universally praised, but the efforts of the other attorneys received mixed reviews. Most commentators expected the Court to rule against Dred Scott and his family. Predictably, the reaction to the potential of such a decision split generally along partisan lines. Democratic newspapers typically looked forward hopefully to a final settlement of the dispute over slavery in the territories. By contrast, Republicans such as Horace Greeley complained that a Court with a majority of Southern justices was hardly in a position to issue an impartial decision on the issue of slavery in the territories.

The deliberations of the Court were delayed after the wife of Justice Peter V. Daniel was burned to death in a horrible accident on January 3, 1857. Daniel, who himself suffered minor burns in the incident, was understandably grief-stricken and did not attend another session of Court until the middle of February. Accordingly, *Dred Scott* was not considered by the full Court in conference until February 14. Before the first conference, the Court seemed poised to issue a narrow decision. On February 3, James Buchanan wrote to his friend Justice John Catron, asking whether the Court would hand down a decision in *Dred Scott* to which Buchanan should refer in his upcoming inaugural address. After first telling Buchanan that the Court had not yet reached a decision, on February 10 Catron wrote the president-elect that the Court would probably decide the case at the February 14 conference and that the Court would probably not reach the issue of the constitutionality of prohibiting slavery in the territories.

This judgment was initially vindicated at the February 14 conference. First, Samuel Nelson, who earlier had been inclined to the view that the issue of Scott's citizenship was properly before the Court, changed his mind and joined Catron, John McLean, Robert Grier, and John Campbell to create a majority supporting the view that the objection to jurisdiction had been waived. Second, although some of the Southern justices may have preferred a broad opinion even at this stage, the majority concluded that the case should be decided against the Scott family on grounds that did not require discussion of the constitutionality of the Missouri Compromise. Instead, Nelson was assigned the task of writing an opinion that concluded that, under *Strader v. Graham*, the status of the Scotts was determined by Missouri state law, and that the Court was bound to follow the ruling in *Scott v. Emerson*.

Even if Nelson's approach had ultimately been accepted by a majority of the justices, some discussion of the more explosive issues presented by *Dred Scott* would likely have ensued. As early as February 6, Justice Catron predicted in a letter to President Buchanan that Justice Daniel intended to deliver a long opinion in the case. Given Daniel's political perspective, such an opinion would no doubt have included a vigorous assault on the constitutionality of the Missouri Compromise. Conversely, the most obvious course of argument for any justice who was inclined to hold in favor of the Scotts required a discussion of the Missouri Compromise. A judgment against the Scotts could have been based simply on a decision to defer to the Missouri Supreme Court on the issue of Missouri law, but a decision in favor of Harriet required a finding that she had become free during her time at Fort Snelling. In the absence of some legal sleight-of-hand, this conclusion could be reached only if slavery was in fact illegal in the Wisconsin Territory, a notion that in turn was most plausibly based on the view that Congress had the authority to adopt the Missouri Compromise. While Curtis might have been politically and temperamentally inclined to craft a solution that would have avoided this conclusion, McLean was less likely to feel similarly constrained. But at the very least, antislavery Northerners would have been spared the indignity of having the Court as an *institution* enlisted against their cause.

However, Nelson was not destined to become the spokesman for the *Dred Scott* Court. Sometime prior to November 19, while Nelson was writing his opinion, the deliberations took a sharply different turn. On the motion of Justice James Moore Wayne, the Southern justices united around the view that Chief Justice Taney should write a majority opinion addressing the constitutional issues raised by restrictions on slavery in the land acquired in the Louisiana Purchase.

Wayne's motivation in making this motion has been a matter of great debate. Within ten days of the decision to base the judgment on broad rather than narrow grounds, Catron and Grier had written separately to President Buchanan, each asserting that Wayne had acted in response to a realization that at least one dissent would address the issues of African American citizenship and the constitutionality of the Missouri Compromise. On the other hand, thirteen years later Campbell stated that Wayne had reached his decision independently in the belief that the final resolution of the dispute over slavery in the territories was necessary for the good of the country and that a broad decision by the Court was the only way such a resolution could be achieved. Curtis is reported to have given a similar explanation in a private conversation in 1873. Curtis and McLean also purportedly insisted that an explicit decision overturning the Missouri Compromise could only inflame Northern opinion. The question of which of these accounts is correct has been debated widely in the vast literature analyzing *Dred Scott.* But for whatever reason, the Southerners on the Court became firmly committed to expressing their viewpoint on the constitutional issue.

At this stage in the proceedings, the Southerners turned their attention to persuading Grier to join them. On February 19 Catron once again wrote to Buchanan, informing him that a broad decision was forthcoming and asking him to urge Grier to join the majority on this point. Buchanan wrote to Grier with such a request, and, after consulting Taney and Wayne, Grier agreed, declaring in a February 23 letter to Buchanan that "I am anxious that it should not appear that the line of latitude should mark the line of division in the court." Thus, in his inaugural address on March 4, Buchanan was able to state with perfect equanimity that

> A difference of opinion has arisen in regard to the point of time when the people of a Territory shall decide [whether to allow slavery] for themselves. This is, happily, a matter of little practical importance. Besides, it is a judicial question, which legitimately belongs to the Supreme Court of the United States, before whom it is now pending and will, it is understood, be speedily and finally settled. To their decision, in common with all good citizens I shall cheerfully submit, whatever this may be.

Neither Buchanan nor the country at large would have to wait long for the decision to which he referred. Moreover, the decision did indeed prove to be one to which Buchanan and his allies could "cheerfully submit."

CHAPTER 8

The Opinions of the Justices

Once the decision to address the broader issues presented by *Dred Scott* had been made, Chief Justice Taney assigned to himself the task of writing an opinion for the Court. In addition, with the exception of Justice Grier, all of the other justices took the opportunity to express separate opinions on at least some of the issues presented by the case. Ultimately, seven justices concluded that the Scotts remained slaves, while two believed that Dred Scott and the other members of his family were legally entitled to their freedom.

On March 6, 1857, Chief Justice Taney delivered the majority opinion. He brought to the opinion a commitment to proslavery ideology that, if anything, had intensified since his consideration of *Prigg*. Thus, on the eve of the election of 1856, he fulminated privately about the need for the South to take "firm united action" to "check Northern insult and Northern aggression." However, prior to reaching the question of the constitutionality of the Missouri Compromise, Taney first had to deal with the jurisdictional issues raised by Scott's assertion of jurisdiction based on diversity of citizenship.

Taney began by discussing the procedural posture of the claim that the case should be dismissed for want of diversity of citizenship. He conceded that in an ordinary common-law court, a decision to defend on the merits would have effectively waived all jurisdictional objections. However, he argued that the rule should be different in federal court. Taney observed that jurisdiction is ordinarily presumed to lie in common-law courts. By contrast, he noted, plaintiffs in federal court were required to affirmatively plead the facts that brought a diversity case within the limits of the subject-matter jurisdiction of the federal courts established by Article III of the Constitution, and that this requirement could not be waived by the opposing party. Thus, Taney concluded that once the existence of jurisdictional facts had been put in issue in the trial court, a decision to defend on the merits did not bar an appellate court from reconsideration of the jurisdictional question.

On the substance of the citizenship question, Taney's argument paralleled the unpublished 1832 opinion that he had prepared as attorney general. He began his discussion of the issue by defining the scope of the inquiry in the most sweeping terms. Declining to consider the possibility that the definition of Article III citizenship might be broader than that of federal citizenship for other purposes under the Constitution, he stated that "the question is . . . Can a negro, whose ancestors were imported into this country and sold as slaves, become a member of the political community formed and brought into existence by the Constitution of the United States and as such become entitled to all the rights, and privileges, and immunities, guarantied by that instrument to the citizen [including] the privilege of suing in a court of the United States?" Taney then differentiated sharply between state citizenship and federal citizenship. He contended that, while a state could declare anyone whom it pleased to be a citizen for its own purposes, the states lacked authority to "introduce a new member into the political community created by the Constitution of the United States." That status, according to Taney, was determined by a federal standard and limited to members of two groups: (1) "every person, every class and description of persons, who were at the time of the adoption of the Constitution recognised as citizens in the several States" and (2) those foreigners whom Congress might choose to naturalize under the authority granted to it by the Constitution.

Taney next turned to an extended historical discussion of the status of free blacks in the late eighteenth century, beginning with his oft-quoted (and misquoted) observation that "they had no rights which the white man was bound to respect." He reasoned that because free blacks lacked fundamental rights at the time the Constitution was adopted, they were not considered citizens at that time. In reaching this conclusion, Taney drew on a number of different sources. First, he argued that the laws of the various states limiting the rights of blacks during the founding period were inconsistent with the status of citizenship. Second, he claimed that the fugitive slave clause and the clause limiting congressional power over the slave trade "point directly and specifically to the negro race as a separate class of persons . . . not regarded as a portion of the . . . citizens of the Government [formed by the Constitution]." Third, he contended that early actions of the federal government seemed to reflect the view that free blacks were not citizens. Finally, he argued that during the founding period, many states would have been unwilling to allow transient black inhabitants from other states the privileges and immunities guaranteed to citizens by the comity clause.

Taney bolstered his argument by emphasizing what he viewed as the undesirable practical consequences of establishing a regime in which free blacks were considered citizens. He contended that if states were required to recognize sojourning blacks as citizens, "[the comity clause] would exempt them from the operation of the special laws [and give them the right] . . . to go where they pleased at every hour of the day or night without molestation, unless they committed some violation of law for which a white man would be punished and . . . the full liberty of speech in public and in private upon all subjects upon which [the state's] own citizens might speak."

Similarly, he later contended that

> if [a person] ranks as a citizen of the State to which he belongs, within the meaning of the Constitution of the United States, then, whenever he goes into another State, the Constitution clothes him, as to the rights of person, with all privileges and immunities which belong to citizens of the State. And if persons of the African race are citizens of a State, and of the United States, they would be entitled to all of these privileges and immunities in every State, and the State could not restrict them; for they would hold these privileges and immunities under the paramount authority of the Federal Government, and its courts would be bound to maintain and enforce them, the Constitution and laws of the State to the contrary notwithstanding.

Based on these historical and practical considerations, Taney concluded that the descendants of slaves could not become citizens of the United States, and that the lower court had erred in declining to dismiss the case for want of jurisdiction.

From a purely legal perspective, the opinion could clearly have stopped at this point, sending the case back to the trial court to be dismissed on jurisdictional grounds. But having determined to reach the question of the Scotts' status, Taney faced another procedural problem. Since he had decided that the federal courts lacked jurisdiction over the lawsuit, it was arguably inappropriate for him to discuss the merits of the case. Taney dealt with this problem by recasting the issue of the status of the Scotts in jurisdictional terms. He noted that if the undisputed facts established that the Scotts were slaves, they could not be citizens, and the federal courts would lack jurisdiction on that ground as well. Although the plea in abatement had not asserted that the Scotts were slaves, Taney contended that the Supreme Court could nonetheless legitimately consider this issue. Distinguishing *Dred Scott* from appeals from state court judgments, Taney asserted that "it is the daily practice of this court, and of all appellate courts where they reverse the judgment of an inferior court for error, to correct by its opinions whatever errors may appear on the record material to the case; and they have always held it to be their duty to do so where the silence of the court might lead to misconstruction or further controversy, and the point has been relied on by either side, and argued before the court."

Not surprisingly, most of Taney's discussion of the Scotts' status focused on the constitutional challenge to the Missouri Compromise. He began with a long discussion of the scope of congressional power under Article IV, Section 3, which vests Congress with the power to "make all needful Rules and Regulations respecting the Territory or other Property belonging to the United States." Taney contended that the territories clause applied only to territory already claimed by the United States at the time the Constitution was ratified and was thus inapplicable to the land acquired through the Louisiana Purchase. Therefore, in Taney's view, the territories clause granted Congress no power to adopt the limitation on slavery in the Missouri Compromise.

In making this argument, Taney was forced to confront the seemingly contrary authority of *American Ocean Insurance Company v. Canter,* in which Chief Justice Marshall had declared that while Florida remained a territory, it was "governed by that clause of the Constitution which empowers Congress to make all needful rules and regulations respecting the territory or other property of the United States" — the territories clause. Since Florida had also been acquired after the ratification of the Constitution, Taney was faced with the problem of explaining why the same principle should not apply to the Louisiana Purchase. He attempted to resolve this difficulty by claiming that this passage had to be read in the context of the entire *Canter* opinion and that other language in the opinion suggested that the scope of the territories clause remained an open question.

Disposing of the textual provision that seemingly granted Congress plenary power over the territories was an important step in Taney's argument. It did not, however, conclusively establish the constitutional case against the Missouri Compromise. Taney expressed the view that Congress had authority "to organize society [in the territories], and to protect the inhabitants in their persons and property"—a power that he viewed as implicit in the power to admit new states granted by Article IV, Section 3, paragraph 1. Moreover, he conceded that Congress had great discretion in determining the proper form of government for each territory. In the absence of some contrary constitutional provision, this implied power should have been sufficient to justify a prohibition on slavery.

Taney's solution to this problem was twofold. First, he made his well-known appeal to the doctrine of substantive due process. Noting that the Fifth Amendment provided that "no person shall . . . be deprived of life, liberty, or property, without due process of law," he argued that "an act of Congress which deprives a citizen of the United States of [his] property, merely because he came himself or brought his property into a particular Territory of the United States, could hardly be dignified with the name of due process of law." Standing alone, this argument is quite weak. Even under Taney's conception of the power of Congress over the territories, the federal government must have had authority to forbid ownership of some types of property whose possession would be legal in some states. Therefore, the protections of the due process clause could be implicated only if slavery had some special constitutional status.

Taney found evidence of this status in the fugitive slave clause and the guarantee of the right of the states to allow the importation of slaves until 1808. In his view, these constitutional provisions demonstrated that "the right of property in a slave is distinctly and expressly affirmed in the Constitution." Moreover, he asserted that "no word can be found in the Constitution which gives Congress a greater power over slave property, or which entitles property of that kind to less protection than property of any other description. The only power conferred is the power coupled with the duty of guarding and protecting the owner in his rights." The special constitutional status of slavery was the linchpin of both Taney's argument and the Southern position on slavery in the territories generally. Taney also invoked the common-property doctrine, declaring that the Louisiana Purchase "was acquired by the General Government, as the representative and trustee of the people of the United States, and it must therefore be held in that character for their common and equal benefit . . . until it shall be associated with the other States as a member of the Union."

Having disposed of the issue of the constitutionality of the Missouri Compromise, Taney then turned to the claim that Dred Scott was free because of his residence in Illinois. Taney left the detailed analysis of this issue to the concurring opinion of Justice Samuel Nelson; his own discussion of this point was so brief as to be almost perfunctory. He simply relied on *Strader v. Graham* and concluded that the Court was bound by the Missouri Supreme Court's decision in *Scott v. Emerson*. Against this background, Taney concluded that Dred Scott and his family remained slaves and therefore could not be citizens. Taney thus concluded that the federal courts could not assert jurisdiction over the case on the basis of diversity of citizenship and that the complaint should have been dismissed on those grounds.

Unlike Taney, Nelson chose to rest entirely on the narrow opinion that he had prepared before his colleagues had decided to address the constitutionality of the Missouri Compromise. Nelson declined to address the issue of whether the descendants of slaves could become citizens of the United States, arguing that the validity of the original plea in abatement was not properly before the Court. Further, while observing that "many of the most eminent statesmen and jurists of the country" had questioned the constitutionality of the Missouri Compromise, in *Dred Scott* he proceeded on the assumption that Congress possessed authority to ban slavery from the territories. Finally, Nelson concluded that the facts demonstrated that Dr. Emerson had not established a domicile in any state or territory in which slavery was outlawed by either state or federal law.

Proceeding from these assumptions, the analysis in Nelson's opinion closely tracked the Court's argument in *Strader*. He began with the commonplace observations that, in general, "every State or nation possesses an exclusive sovereignty and jurisdiction within her territory; and her laws affect and bind all property and persons residing within it" and that "no State . . . can enact laws to operate beyond its own dominions, and, if it attempts to do so, it may be lawfully refused obedience." Thus, in the absence of constitutional limitation, "it belongs to the sovereign State of Missouri to determine by her laws the question of slavery within her jurisdiction, subject only to such limitations as may be found in the Federal Constitution." Relying directly on *Strader*, Nelson then concluded that the power of Congress over slavery in the territories had no constitutionally binding extraterritorial effect, noting that "Congress has no power whatever over the subject of slavery within [a] state" and arguing that to hold otherwise would be "subversive of the established doctrine of international jurisprudence . . . that the laws of one Government have no force within the limits of another."

Nelson then turned to an examination of the law of the state of Missouri itself. He characterized the decision in *Scott v. Emerson* as generally consistent with the overall pattern of state law, contending that, in general, the Missouri cases that had denied operation of the doctrine of reattachment had involved situations in which the master had established a domicile in a free state. The one exception was *Rachel v. Walker*, in which the Missouri courts had held that a slave had gained permanent freedom in a factual situation strikingly similar to that of *Dred Scott*. However, Nelson argued that the state court was free to reexamine the *Rachel* doctrine, and that in any event *Rachel* was contrary to the decisions of other courts that had considered the issue. Thus, Nelson concluded that Scott and his family remained slaves.

Both Grier and Wayne delivered short opinions noting their complete agreement with the conclusions reached by Taney and Nelson. Neither opinion added materially to the analysis of the substantive issues raised by the case. Wayne did, however, launch a spirited defense of the appropriateness of discussing the question of the constitutionality of the Missouri Compromise. Distinguishing sharply between appeals from state courts and lower federal courts, Wayne argued that once the issue of the jurisdiction of the lower federal court was properly placed before the Supreme Court, the Court was empowered to consider the entire record in determining whether the lower court had in fact been authorized to take jurisdiction by the Constitution and the relevant federal statutes.

In contrast to Nelson, Grier, and Wayne, Justices Daniel, Campbell, and Catron filed opinions addressing both the question of the constitutionality of the Missouri Compromise and the larger question of the power of Congress to prohibit slavery in the territories. Each of the three justices joined Taney in concluding that the Missouri Compromise was unconstitutional. However, the arguments they deployed differed significantly from those in the opinion of the chief justice.

The intensity of Daniel's emotional commitment to Southern institutions and interests was reflected in his *Dred Scott* concurrence. From a purely substantive perspective, Daniel's ultimate conclusions were no different from those of Chief Justice Taney. The tone of the concurrence, however, was much more extreme than that of the majority opinion.

Daniel began with a characterization of African Americans that he saw as based upon "truths which a knowledge of the history of the world, and particularly of that of our own country compels us to know," asserting that

> the African negro race never have been acknowledged as belonging to the family of nations; that as amongst them never has been known or recognized by the inhabitants of other countries anything partaking of the character of nationality, or civil or political polity; that this race has been by all the nations of Europe regarded as subjects of capture or purchase; as subjects of commerce; and that the introduction of that race into every section of this country was not as members of civil or political society, but as slaves, as *property* in the strictest sense of the word.

Daniel then argued that neither emancipation per se nor the actions of state governments could transmute slaves into citizens of the United States. He noted that emancipation was simply an act by an individual — the owner of a slave — and that private parties lacked authority to confer the status of citizenship. This conclusion was not particularly noteworthy; however, against the background of his strong commitment to states' rights generally, Daniel's analysis of the relationship between state and federal citizenship is particularly striking:

The States, in the exercise of their political power, might, with reference to their peculiar Government and jurisdiction, guaranty the rights of person and property, and the enjoyment of civil and political privileges, to those whom they should be disposed to make the subjects of their bounty, but they could not reclaim or exert the powers which they had vested exclusively in the United States. They could not add to or change in any respect the class of person to whom alone the character of citizen of the United States appertained at the time of the adoption of the Federal Constitution. They could not create citizens of the United States by any direct or indirect proceeding.

The language of Daniel's opinion became more intemperate as he turned to the question of whether Dred Scott remained a slave. He derided the "vaunted" *Somerset* decision, sarcastically commenting that it was often cited as "the proud evidence of devotion to freedom under a Government which has done as much perhaps to extend the reign of slavery as all the world besides." Turning more specifically to the question of the power of Congress to outlaw slavery in the territories, he relied primarily on the common-property doctrine:

Nothing can be more conclusive to show the equality of [the right to settle in the territories] with every other right in all the citizens of the United States, and the iniquity and absurdity of the pretension to exclude or disfranchise a portion of them because they are the owners of slaves, than the fact that the [Constitution], which imparts to Congress its very existence and every function, guaranties to the slaveholder the right to his property, and gives him the right of reclamation throughout the entire extent of the nation; and farther, that the only private property which the Constitution has *specifically recognized*, and has imposed it as a direct obligation on the States and the Federal Government to protect and *enforce*, is the property of the master in his slave; no other property is placed by the Constitution on the same high ground, nor shielded by a similar guaranty. Can there be imputed to the sages and patriots by whom the Constitution was framed, or can there be detected in the text of the Constitution, or in any rational construction or implication deducible therefrom, a contradiction so palpable as would exist between a pledge to the slaveholder of an equality with his fellow-citizens, and a warrant given . . . to another, to rob him of that property, or to subject him to proscription or disfranchisement for possessing or for endeavoring to retain it? The injustice and extravagance necessarily implied in a supposition like this, cannot be rationally imputed to the patriotic or honest, or to those who were merely sane.

In sharp contrast to the tone of Daniel's concurrence, Campbell's opinion was a measured defense of the states'-rights arm of proslavery constitutionalism distilled to a precise, lawyerly argument. Campbell eschewed any discussion of the issue of the citizenship of free blacks, beginning instead with an analysis of the status of Dred Scott under state law. Campbell appeared to concede that if Scott's master had in fact become a domiciliary of a free state, Scott could have been permanently emancipated through the operation of that state's law. However, Campbell argued that in *Dred Scott* there was no evidence that the master had in fact established a domicile in either Illinois or Minnesota. From this perspective, although taking the opportunity to extensively criticize *Somerset*, Campbell ultimately characterized this aspect of the decision in *Scott v. Emerson* as a perfectly orthodox application of the doctrine of reattachment recognized in *The Slave, Grace*.

Turning to the issue of the constitutionality of the Missouri Compromise, Campbell, like Taney, began by arguing that the territories clause granted Congress only limited authority — in Campbell's words, the power to take "such administrative and conservatory acts as are necessary for the preservation of the public domain, and its preparation for sale or disposition." In particular, he argued that

> whatever [the states'] Constitution and laws validly determine to be property, it is the duty of the Federal Government, through the domain of jurisdiction merely Federal, to recognise to be property. . . . This principle follows from the structure of the respective governments, State and Federal, and their reciprocal relations. They are different agents and trustees of the people of the several States, appointed with different powers and distinct purposes, but whose acts, within the scope of their respective jurisdictions, are mutually obligatory. They are respectively the depositories of such powers of legislation as the people were willing to surrender, and their duty is to co-operate within their several jurisdictions to maintain the

rights of the same citizens under both Governments unimpaired. A proscription, therefore, of the Constitution and laws of one or more States, determining property, on the part of the Federal Government, by which the stability of its social system may be endangered, is plainly repugnant to the conditions on which the Federal Constitution was adopted, or which that Government was designed to accomplish.

Since the Missouri Compromise was unconstitutional, Campbell concluded that Scott remained a slave, and as such was not entitled to maintain a suit in federal court pursuant to diversity of citizenship.

Interestingly, however, Campbell specifically limited his discussion to the constitutionality of congressional enactments. He explicitly refused to comment on the powers of territorial legislatures, suggesting that the judiciary lacked the competence to determine the limits of such bodies' power. Thus, although Campbell had nothing but contempt for the doctrine of popular sovereignty in political terms, unlike Taney, he suggested that the people of the territories themselves possessed the authority to ban slavery.

John Catron's opinion clearly reflected the impact of the political developments of the 1850s on American politics in general and Southern politics in particular. In 1848 Catron had privately advocated the extension of the Missouri Compromise line to the Pacific and declared that if he were a member of Congress, he would have voted to exclude slavery from Oregon. Catron no doubt viewed this approach as a means to permanently resolve the territorial issue on a relatively amicable basis, much as the supporters of the Missouri Compromise had believed that they had found a means to remove the irritant of the territorial issue from national politics. However, like Wayne, Catron apparently concluded that, in the wake of the passage of the Kansas-Nebraska Act and the rise of the Republican Party, only the constitutionalization of the Southern position could still the ongoing disruptions in American politics generated by the territorial question.

Despite this conclusion, Catron's opinion took a quite different tack than those of his Southern brethren. At the outset, Catron flatly refused to entertain the question of Scott's citizenship, concluding that any objection to the jurisdiction of the Court had been waived by the choice to actively defend on the merits. In addition, he rejected Taney's claim that the territories clause was not by its terms broad enough to empower Congress to outlaw slavery in the territories under its control. Nonetheless, Catron ultimately concluded that the Missouri Compromise violated the rights of slaveowners who wished to bring their property into the northern portion of the Louisiana Purchase.

Catron based this conclusion on two separate arguments. First, he cited a provision of the treaty of cession itself, which provided that, until "incorporated into the Union," "the inhabitants of the [Louisiana] territory . . . shall be maintained and protected in the free enjoyment of their liberty, property, and the religion which they possess." Noting that slavery was well established in the Louisiana territory at the time of the cession, Catron argued that this provision protected the right to hold slaves not only of those resident in the territory in 1803 but also of those who moved into the territory subsequent to its purchase by the United States.

Taken alone, this argument would have left the issue of slavery in the Mexican Cession untouched. However, Catron also vigorously defended the common-property doctrine, contending that it was embodied in the comity clause. Rejecting the almost universally accepted view that the clause simply guaranteed that citizens in state A who found themselves in state B would have the same fundamental rights as citizens in state B, Catron instead contended that "the [meaning of] the cited clause is not that citizens of the United States shall have equal privileges in the Territories, but the citizen of each State shall come there in right of his State, and enjoy the common property. He secures his equality through the equality of his State, by virtue of that great fundamental condition of the Union — the equality of the States." Thus, while not agreeing with the reasoning in the Taney, Campbell, and Daniel opinions, Catron concluded that Congress could not constitutionally ban slavery from the territories.

Justices John McLean and Benjamin Robbins Curtis both disagreed sharply with Taney on virtually every issue presented in *Dred Scott*. However, their opinions were as different in tone as those of Daniel and Campbell. When he believed that the *Dred Scott* decision would be handed down before the Republican Convention in June 1856, McLean had informed his supporters that he had prepared an opinion that would allay fears about his commitment to the antislavery cause and improve his standing among more radical elements of the party. Although the decision in the case was postponed until 1857, well after Fremont had gained the Republican nomination and Buchanan had won the general election, McLean apparently did not alter the wording of his dissent (perhaps looking to another potential run at the Republican nomination in 1860). Thus, the opinion combined orthodox legal analysis with political rhetoric calculated to convince radical Republicans that McLean was an acceptable standard-bearer for the party.

McLean began by making short work of the jurisdictional argument. He first expressed the view that the question of Scott's citizenship was not properly before the Court. However, assuming for the purpose of argument that the issue should be addressed on the merits, McLean adopted the most advanced Republican position on this point, declaring that "the most general and appropriate definition of the term citizen is 'a freeman.' Being a freeman, and having his domicil [sic] in a state different from that of the defendant, [Scott] is a citizen . . . and the courts of the Union are open to him."

Not surprisingly, the bulk of the opinion was devoted to the issue of slavery in the territories. McLean began his argument on this point by asserting that, at the time the Constitution was drafted, "it is a well-known fact that a belief was cherished by the leading men, South as well as North, that the institution of slavery would gradually decline, until it would become extinct." He then reiterated the basic premise of antislavery constitutionalism, asserting that "all slavery has its origins in power, and is against right." Against this background, McLean reiterated the argument that he initially had made in 1847, declaring that "there is no power in the Constitution by which Congress can make either white men or black men slaves."

Of course, in *Dred Scott* itself, the only issue was whether Congress could constitutionally *bar* slavery from the territories. Thus, McLean was able to take a position that, although in some tension with the views he had expressed in 1847, was nonetheless more consistent with his basic nationalist perspective. Characterizing the Court's opinion in *Canter* as dispositive, he emphatically rejected Taney's contention that Chief Justice Marshall's sweeping vindication of congressional power to govern the territories in that case was dictum. Analogizing *Dred Scott* to *Canter*, McLean concluded that "if Congress may establish a Territorial Government in the exercise of its discretion, it is a clear principle that a court cannot control that discretion. This being the case, I do not see on what ground the act is held to be void. It did not purport to forfeit property, or take it for public purposes. It only prohibited slavery; in doing which, it followed the ordinance of 1787."

Having disposed of the claim that the Missouri Compromise was unconstitutional, McLean then sought to refute the contention that the Court was bound to respect the Missouri court's conclusion that Scott was a slave under Missouri law. In substantial measure, McLean's disagreement with Nelson was based upon a different characterization of Emerson's status in Illinois. Nelson viewed Emerson as little more than a mere sojourner in Illinois, but McLean contended that Emerson had acquired a domicile in that state. Proceeding from this premise, McLean concluded that the Missouri decision was inconsistent with both common law and constitutional principles.

On the common-law issue, McLean argued that the state court decision was contrary not only to international law and the decided cases from other jurisdictions, but also to the prior decisions of the Missouri Supreme Court itself. McLean appeared to concede that, absent constitutional considerations, the U.S. Supreme Court would have been required to acquiesce in the enforcement of a state *statute* that abrogated the common law on this point. However, he noted that in *Pease v. Peck* Justice Grier had spoken for the Court in establishing the principle that "when the decisions of the State court are not consistent, we do not feel bound to follow the last, if it is contrary to our own convictions; and much more is the case where, after a long course of consistent decisions, some new light suddenly springs up, or an excited public opinion has elicited new doctrines subversive of former safe precedent." Given his antislavery sentiments, McLean had no trouble in concluding that this precedent justified reversal of the decision of the Missouri court.

This argument alone would have provided a sufficient basis for holding that Dred Scott should be released from bondage. Nonetheless, McLean went further, contending that Scott could not constitutionally be returned to slavery in Missouri. McLean founded this conclusion on considerations of horizontal federalism. He argued that the Missouri courts were constitutionally bound to respect the change in status worked by the constitution of Illinois, declaring:

The States of Missouri and Illinois are bounded by a common line. The one prohibits slavery, the other admits it. This has been done by the exercise of that sovereign power that appertains to each. We are bound to respect the institutions of each, as emanating from the voluntary action of the people. . . . I am unable to reconcile [the Missouri judgment] with the respect due to the State of Illinois. Having the same rights of sovereignty as the State of Missouri in adopting a Constitution, I can perceive no reason why the institutions of Illinois should not receive the same consideration as those of Missouri.

Throughout McLean's opinion, the legal analysis was interspersed with seemingly gratuitous assaults on the institution of slavery itself. For example, McLean asserted that "we need not refer to the mercenary spirit in slaves, to show the degradation of Negro slavery in our country," and that "a slave is not a mere chattel. He bears the impress of his Maker, and is amenable to the laws of God and man." Similarly, in responding to the Southern claim that slavery must be allowed in the territories because the territories were the "common property" of the states, McLean turned the argument on its head, declaring that "the repugnance to slavery would probably prevent fifty or a hundred freemen from settling in a slave territory, where one slaveholder would be prevented from settling in a free Territory." In short, taken as a whole, McLean's opinion was no less extreme or provocative than that of Peter Daniel.

Curtis's dissent was far more moderate in tone. On the citizenship issue, Curtis steered a middle course. He first took issue with Taney's reading of history, contending that at least five states granted free blacks citizenship at the time the Constitution was drafted. Under the Articles of Confederation, these blacks would have been entitled to the privileges and immunities of national citizenship. Thus, for Curtis, the question was whether the Constitution had deprived free blacks of their right to citizenship. After noting that the Constitution by its terms did not define national citizenship, he expressly considered three other possibilities — that Congress possessed the authority to define citizenship, that all free persons born within the United States were to be considered citizens of the United States, and that each state was to be free to determine "what free persons, born within its limits, shall be citizens of such State, and *thereby* citizens of the United States."

Curtis rejected the first possibility on both practical and doctrinal grounds. He initially observed that if Congress possessed such a power, it could unduly circumscribe the class of persons eligible to be president, vice president, or a member of Congress simply by narrowly defining the term "citizen of the United States." In addition, he noted that the Constitution does not specifically grant Congress general authority to define citizenship; the only directly relevant provision provides that Congress shall have power "to establish a uniform rule of *naturalization*" — a term that, in Curtis's view, was limited to the removal of the disabilities of alienage from persons of foreign birth. Therefore, the doctrine of enumerated powers also militated against the theory that Congress had unfettered authority to grant or withhold national citizenship.

Curtis was thus left with a choice between McLean's position — that all native-born free persons were citizens — and the conclusion that each state had the authority to decide (at least as an initial matter) which of its native-born residents should be considered citizens of the United States. In defending the latter theory, Curtis relied in part on a textual argument. He observed that the comity clause provides that "citizens of each *State* shall be entitled to all the privileges and immunities of citizens of the several States" — in effect, choosing state citizenship as the benchmark for the determination that a person was entitled to national protection for the rights appurtenant to that status.

Primarily, however, Curtis grounded his conclusion in fundamental principles of constitutional interpretation. He noted that prior to the adoption of the Constitution, each state had possessed the authority to define citizenship as an inherent aspect of its sovereign authority. Further, the states retained all aspects of sovereign authority not granted to the federal government by the Constitution. Since only the power of naturalization was granted to Congress, in Curtis's view the states retained authority to determine the status of native-born residents.

Although he rejected Taney's extreme proslavery approach, Curtis's analysis of the citizenship question fell far short of advanced antislavery positions. First, under his theory, if a black person was born in a state that did not consider him a citizen, he could *never* obtain that status. States clearly did not possess the power to confer national citizenship on persons born outside their borders. Moreover, Curtis repeatedly emphasized that federal power over naturalization extended only to aliens — those born outside the boundaries of the United States. Thus, while in theory Congress could have granted U.S. citizenship to a native African who emigrated to the United States, the federal government was powerless to take similar action with respect to a person who was born a slave in South Carolina and was later emancipated in Massachusetts.

Further, under Curtis's analysis the Constitution guaranteed only limited rights to those free blacks who were in fact citizens of the United States. Clearly, as citizens they would be entitled to invoke the jurisdiction of the federal courts on the ground of diversity of citizenship, and to be candidates for president, vice president, and Congress. The comity clause also guaranteed citizens of the United States the right to free ingress and egress to and from all states in the Union — a right that was denied by the Negro Seamen's Acts. The question of what other rights free black citizens would enjoy, however, was to be in considerable measure a function of state law.

Curtis clearly adopted the dominant view of the comity clause, which both limited the scope of the interests subject to the privileges and immunities clause and, in many cases, defined the rights of sojourners by reference to those granted by the state to its own citizens. Under this view, if a state imposed some racial restriction on its own black citizens, it could impose a similar restriction on blacks from other states. Thus, responding to the argument that, under his approach, states such as South Carolina would be required to allow free blacks from (for example) Massachusetts to vote and hold office, Curtis first contended that these rights were not protected by the comity clause. He continued, "Privileges and immunities which belong to certain citizens of a State, by reason of the operation of causes other than mere citizenship, are not conferred. . . . It rests with the States themselves so to frame their Constitutions and laws as not to attach a particular privilege or immunity to mere naked citizenship. If one of the State will not deny to any of its citizens a particular privilege or immunity, if it confer it on all of them by reason of mere naked citizenship, then it may be claimed by every citizen of each State by force of the Constitution."

This analysis clearly indicates that states that granted free blacks citizenship could nonetheless place race-based restrictions on the rights of all blacks — whether domiciliaries or sojourners. Suppose, however, that a state restricted citizenship to white domiciliaries. Could it then deny to black citizens from other states a fundamental right that it granted to all white, native-born citizens — for example, the right to buy real property? Although Curtis did not give a definitive answer to this question, the language of his opinion suggests that no such discrimination would be constitutional under the comity clause.

This conclusion was not a reflection of any particular solicitude for the rights of free blacks per se. It was simply a logical corollary to the same vision of federalism that underlay Curtis's approach to the issue of fugitive slaves. From his perspective, in both cases the Constitution assigned to a single state the authority to make an initial determination regarding status; in the case of national citizenship, that state was the individual's place of birth, and in the case of the master-slave relationship, the relevant state was that of the owner's domicile. From the perspective of other states, the Constitution also assigned a relatively limited significance to that initial determination; under the comity clause, states were required only to provide citizens from other states with the rights common to all state citizens, and under the fugitive slave clause, the state was required to recognize only the owner's claims to recovery of fugitives, as opposed to slaves brought voluntarily into the state. Within the limited scope of the constitutional protection, however, states were not allowed to interfere, whether through the Negro Seamen's Acts or personal liberty laws. The same symmetry of argument would mark Curtis's treatment of the subconstitutional issues of comity implicated by the ultimate determination of the status of Dred Scott.

Curtis first took direct issue with the majority's decision to reach the merits at all. Observing that the plea in abatement had not challenged Dred Scott's citizenship on the ground that he was a slave, Curtis argued that this omission left the Supreme Court without the power to reach the issue once it had found that the Court lacked jurisdiction for other reasons. Curtis asserted that "a great question of constitutional law, deeply affecting the peace and welfare of the country, is not . . . a fit subject to be thus reached" and also declared that "I do not hold any opinion of this court . . . binding, when expressed on a question [such as this] not legitimately before it." At the same time, Curtis argued that, because he believed that Court *did* have jurisdiction, he was compelled to discuss the merits of the case.

On the substantive question, he took issue with virtually all of the arguments of the majority. Curtis described the territories clause as "a power to pass all needful laws respecting [the territories]" and declared that "whatever Congress deems needful is so, under the grant of power." At the same time, he recognized that the scope of the territories clause was not in fact the central issue in the case. As already noted, unless limited by some extrinsic constitutional provision, Congress would have had authority to prohibit slavery in the territories even under Taney's limited view of congressional power. Thus, Curtis dealt extensively with Taney's due process argument.

On this point, Curtis began with the basic antislavery view of the institution of slavery, echoing the language Justice Joseph Story had used in *Prigg:* "Slavery, being contrary only to natural right, is created only by municipal law." Further, Curtis noted that because slavery defined a status, the precise powers, duties, and obligations that grow out of that status must also be defined by municipal law. Thus, in Curtis's view, Taney's argument implied that the Constitution created an anomaly, protecting the institution of slavery in the abstract but not defining the incidents of the status that are an integral part of the institution.

Curtis contended that the common-property doctrine created an even more troubling anomaly, allowing the rights of citizens of slave states in the territories to be judged by one set of municipal regulations and the rights of citizens from free states to be governed by another. Though agreeing that the territories were acquired for the common benefit of all the people of the United States, Curtis argued that the common benefit was to be defined collectively rather than individually, and that Congress had the authority to determine how best to administer the territories. He concluded his critique of the common property doctrine by declaring that "whatever individual claims may be found on local circumstances, or sectional differences of condition, cannot, in my opinion, be recognised in this court, without arrogating to the judicial branch of the Government powers not committed to it; and which . . . I do not think it fitted to wield."

Curtis thus clearly rejected the proslavery arguments advanced by Taney and the other members of the *Dred Scott* majority. The opinion did not, however, embrace the position espoused by the Republican platform: that the due process clause *prohibited* Congress from granting legal protection to slavery in the territories. Although it was unnecessary for Curtis to directly address the Republican position in his *Dred Scott* opinion, his argument against the common-property doctrine plainly implied that Curtis would have rejected the antislavery analysis as well. In essence, Curtis's position was that the Constitution did not adopt sectional views on the issue of slavery in the territories; instead, it was left to the "best judgment and discretion of the Congress" to choose from among competing perspectives. This analysis was no more consistent with the Republican position than with the common-property doctrine. Curtis's view was that the Constitution was simply neutral on the question of slavery in the territories — a position that by 1857 could appropriately be described as neither antislavery nor proslavery.

Curtis then turned to an examination of the status of Dred Scott after he had returned to Missouri. Curtis began this part of the opinion with an assessment of the impact of the laws of the Wisconsin Territory on the status of the Scotts. He concluded that those laws did not simply deny recognition to slavery but absolutely prohibited the existence of the institution within the territory. Thus, he reasoned that under Wisconsin territorial law, Scott's status was that of a free man. The central question was whether Missouri would recognize that change in status.

At one point, Curtis argued that Missouri was constitutionally required to recognize Scott as a free man. Focusing specifically on Scott's marriage to Harriet, Curtis argued that this marriage was valid under the laws of the Wisconsin Territory and that in any event Emerson's consent had validated the marriage and effectively emancipated Scott. Curtis noted further that the validity of a marriage is governed by the law of the place at which it was contracted, and that the claim that Scott had become a slave once again upon his return to Missouri was inconsistent with the continued validity of the contract of marriage.

Thus, Curtis concluded that for Missouri to consider Scott a slave would not only be "inconsistent with good faith and sound reason, as well as with the rules of international law," but would also violate the prohibition against impairing the obligation of contract contained in Article I, Section 10, clause 1 of the Constitution.

Most of this portion of the Curtis opinion, however, was devoted to establishing the proposition that Scott's travels had rendered him a free man under the common law. At one point Curtis seemed to suggest that, under the principles established in *Swift v. Tyson*, the question was to be decided under federal common law. However, his primary argument, like McLean's, was that the Scotts should have been declared free *under the law of Missouri*. Curtis asserted that because *Scott v. Emerson* was inconsistent with earlier Missouri Supreme Court decisions, he was not required to treat *Emerson* as an authoritative exposition of Missouri law. Instead, he analyzed the relevant state law issues as if the Missouri courts had never addressed them.

Curtis began with the proposition that, in general, only the domicile of a person has the authority to determine his status, and to have that determination recognized by other jurisdictions. He argued that, given the procedural posture in which *Dred Scott* was litigated, Emerson (and thus Scott) should be deemed to have been domiciled in Wisconsin during Emerson's military service there. Moreover, Curtis also argued that in this case technical domicile was not necessary because Emerson was a citizen of the United States, residing in a territory of the United States for an indefinite period of time while conducting the business of the United States. Under these circumstances, Curtis concluded, under generally accepted principles of international law, Missouri should have recognized the change in status generated by Wisconsin law.

He conceded that the state of Missouri could have affirmatively chosen to depart from that principle if it had chosen to do so. He distinguished sharply, however, between the authority of the state itself and that of the state *courts*, arguing that "the judges have nothing to do with the motive of the State. Their duty is simply to ascertain and give effect to its will." Although a state court could depart from international law if required to do so by either statute or "customary" law, it could not adopt a new rule because of "any political considerations, or any view it may take of the exterior political relations between the

State and one or more foreign States, or any impressions it may have that a change of foreign opinion and action on the subject of slavery may afford a reason why the State should change its own action." Since Missouri had adopted the common law (and with it, international law) by statute, in Curtis's view *Emerson* had simply been wrongly decided.

In terms of pure legal analysis, Curtis's refusal to give controlling effect to *Scott v. Emerson* was somewhat dubious. As Taney noted in the majority opinion, under the view taken by the dissenters, any litigant could avoid the strictures of *Strader v. Graham* through the simple expedient of dismissing a state court action prior to judgment and beginning anew in federal court. At the same time, Curtis clearly had the better of the argument on the larger constitutional questions presented by *Dred Scott*. However, because of the nature of these questions, the reaction to the decision was not determined by the strength of the legal analysis in the opinions. Instead, the reaction of different factions was dictated by the same political forces that shaped the larger debate over sectional relations generally and slavery in the territories in particular.

CHAPTER 9

The Impact of *Dred Scott*

After the Supreme Court's decision, Dred Scott and his family faded into obscurity. In May 1857 their ownership was transferred to Taylor Blow, the son of Peter Blow, who immediately freed them. The family lived in Saint Louis, with Dred working as a hotel porter and Harriet as a laundress. Dred died of tuberculosis on September 17, 1858. The subsequent fate of the other members of the family is unclear.

By contrast, the impact of *Dred Scott* on the Court and the political system was anything but obscure. Almost immediately after the decision was handed down, the circumstances surrounding the publication of the opinions in *Dred Scott* created a rift between Chief Justice Taney and Justice Curtis. The chain of events leading to the rift began with the decision by Justice Curtis to immediately release a copy of his dissenting opinion to the representative of a Boston newspaper who had requested it. Curtis later claimed to have been acting on the belief that Taney, like Curtis, had already filed a copy of his opinion with the clerk of the court and that this opinion was also available for public distribution. Taney, however, had not yet filed his opinion, and the dissemination of the principal dissent thus provided the opponents of the *Dred Scott* decision with an enormous advantage in the propaganda battle that erupted immediately after the case was decided.

Taney did not file his opinion immediately because, contrary to the established practice of the Court, he was busily revising it to bolster his argument against some of the criticisms levied by Curtis in his dissent delivered from the bench. While denying that he had altered his original opinion to include "any one [new] historical fact, principle, or point of law," Taney later admitted to Curtis that the revised majority opinion included "[additional] proofs and authorities to maintain the truth of the historical facts and principles asserted by the court in the [majority] opinion delivered from the bench, but which were denied in the dissenting opinions." Curtis later estimated that the revised opinion contained more than eighteen pages of material that had not been in the majority opinion that Taney had delivered in Court on March 6. By the end of March, rumors that Taney was revising his opinion had reached Curtis. Worried that his dissent might need to be changed in order to respond to the revisions in the majority opinion, on April 2 Curtis wrote to William T. Carroll, the clerk of the Supreme Court, asking to be provided with a copy of Taney's opinion as soon as it was printed. On April 6 Carroll responded that he had been instructed by Taney not to provide anyone with a copy of the chief justice's opinion before it appeared in the official reports. On April 9 Curtis wrote again, suggesting that the order could not possibly have been intended to apply to him. On April 14 Carroll responded that Taney himself had confirmed that no copy of the opinion should be provided to Curtis.

Between April 28 and June 20 Curtis and Taney exchanged an increasingly frosty set of letters on the subject of the clerk's refusal to provide Curtis with a copy of Taney's opinion. During this exchange, Taney's language was particularly intemperate. Taney contended that Curtis should have obtained the permission of the other justices before releasing his dissent to the press, complaining bitterly that "no one could fail to see that [the release of Curtis's opinion alone] would encourage attacks upon the court and the [other] judges who gave [different opinions] by political partisans whose prejudices and passions were already enlisted against the constitutional principles affirmed by the court." In addition, obviously stung by Curtis's assertion that Taney's discussion of the constitutionality of the Missouri Compromise was not binding, Taney first suggested that Curtis did not actually wish to see the opinion for any reason related to his official duties but rather "for some other unexplained purpose," which Taney implied was to convey the opinion to Charles P. Curtis, Justice Curtis's former law partner, whose initial request for a copy of the opinion of the Court had occasioned Taney's directive that it not be released until published in the official reports. By June 20 it was clear that the rift between the two justices was irreparable. Although financial concerns also played a role, the unpleasant exchange with Taney no doubt influenced Curtis's decision to resign from the Court on September 1.

In the country at large, initial responses to *Dred Scott* broke down along predictable partisan lines. Republicans excoriated the majority. The *New York Daily Tribune* condemned the decision as "wicked" and "abominable" and denounced the "cunning chief" whose "collation of statements and shallow sophistries" showed a "detestable hypocrisy" and a "mean and skulking cowardice." The *Independent* was equally unsparing in its criticism of *Dred Scott*, describing the decision as "a deliberate, willful perversion, for a particular purpose" and "a vain attempt to change the law by the power of Judges who have achieved only their own infamy" and declaring, "If the people obey this decision, they disobey God." Similarly, the *Ohio State Journal* characterized the Court's conclusions as "palpable perversions of the views of the Fathers of the Republic"; the Chicago *Democratic-Press* evinced "a feeling of shame and loathing" for "this once illustrious tribunal, toiling meekly and patiently through this dirty job"; and the Chicago *Tribune* asserted that "we scarcely know how to express our detestation of [*Dred Scott's*] inhuman dicta, or to fathom the wicked consequences which may flow from it." Sen. William Pitt Fessenden of Maine summarized the views of Republicans generally when he proclaimed that "[the] opinion [of the Court], if carried into practice, undermines the institutions of the country."

Conversely, Democrats of all stripes at first hailed the decision as a decisive repudiation of the political creed of the rival Republicans. Northern Democrats greeted the decision with enthusiasm. For example, the *Illinois State Register* declared that "the people who revere the Constitution and the laws . . . will hail the decision with satisfaction." Sounding a similar note, the *New York Journal of Commerce* asserted that the decision "dissipates the mist in which we have been enveloped for years; it exposes in all their deformities the slavery heresies by which we have been disturbed for more than a half a century."

Not surprisingly, Southerners were even more ebullient. The *Richmond Daily Enquirer* cheered that "*sectionalism* has been rebuked, and abolitionism has been staggered and stunned," and the *Nashville Union and American* asserted that *Dred Scott* "fully and completely vindicates and sustains the Democratic party in the patriotism and wisdom of its course throughout the entire history of slavery agitation" and that "now every Department of the Government has sanctioned our views, and the principles of the Kansas Nebraska Act has [sic] been sanctioned by a majority of Congress, a Northern President and Northern Judges of the Supreme Court." Similarly, the *New Orleans Picayune* claimed with satisfaction that *Dred Scott* "puts the whole basis of the Black Republican organization under the ban of law, stamps its designs as hostile to the Constitution, and forms the basis upon which all conservative men of the Union can unite for the maintenance of the Constitution as it is and the Union as it is." At the same time, a number of Southern commentators warned against overestimating the significance of their triumph in the Supreme Court. Noting continuing Republican defiance, the *Charleston Mercury* admonished Southerners not to "cherish the delusion that [their] cause is triumphant and [their] rights secure," warning that "the Abolitionists are not at all abashed or dismayed; on the contrary, they accept this repulse as another blow in the work of imparting compactness and strength to their organization, and from the fire that consumes *Dred Scott*, they appear to anticipate a conflagration that will again set the popular sentiment of the North in a blaze of indignation." The *Mercury* also accurately predicted that "the Black Republican party will go into the [presidential election] of 1860, strengthened rather than discredited and weakened by the adverse judgment of the Supreme Court."

What the *Mercury* did not predict was that *Dred Scott* would ultimately have a divisive impact on the Democratic Party itself. The source of the problem lay in the underlying difference of opinion between Northern and Southern Democrats on the issue of slavery in the territories. Whereas Northern Democrats generally hewed to the concept of popular sovereignty, Southerners more often adopted the version of the "nonintervention" theory that would effectively have allowed slavery in all of the territories. Prior to the decision in *Dred Scott*, the two wings of the party had agreed to disagree on the issue of the constitutionality of prohibitions on slavery by territorial legislatures.

The specific issue that divided Democrats had not been raised by the facts of *Dred Scott*. Nonetheless, although Campbell had explicitly concluded that the courts should not overturn territorial legislative actions, Taney had stated that such legislation was unconstitutional, and the logic of the arguments of Daniel and Catron seemed to lead to the same conclusion. Although Taney's discussion of the issue was clearly dictum, Southerners took the view that *Dred Scott* had vindicated their position.

This conclusion was anathema to many Northern Democrats, who remained firmly committed to the doctrine of popular sovereignty. The sectional divide within the party would assume greater importance as the debate over *Dred Scott* became subsumed in a renewed struggle over the fate of Kansas.

In February 1857—one month before Buchanan took office and the Supreme Court decided *Dred Scott*—the Kansas territorial legislature, still dominated by proslavery politicians, passed legislation designed to pave the way for the admission of Kansas to the Union. The legislation called for a census to be held in March, an election of delegates to a constitutional convention in June, and a convention in September. By this time antislavery forces were clearly in the majority in Kansas. Nonetheless, fearing that the process would be conducted unfairly to their detriment, free staters decided to boycott the election.

To deal with this explosive situation, Buchanan appointed Robert J. Walker of Pennsylvania to be the territorial governor of Kansas. Based on his background, one might have thought Walker would be sympathetic to Southern interests. Walker was a former Mississippi slaveowner who had served as a senator from that state from 1835 to 1845 and secretary of the treasury to James K. Polk from 1845 to 1849. He had also written one of the most influential tracts advocating the annexation of Texas in 1844. However, soon after assuming the governorship of Kansas, Walker publicly took positions that infuriated the political leadership of the slave states. He asserted that, for geographical reasons, Kansas was destined to be a free state and that Congress would under no circumstances admit Kansas as a slave state or a free state unless "a majority of the people of Kansas shall have fairly and freely decided [the question of slavery] by a direct vote on the adoption of the Constitution, excluding fraud and violence." Despite these comments, antislavery residents of Kansas remained determined to boycott the June elections for delegates to the constitutional convention. As a result, the convention was dominated by supporters of slavery.

The convention that met in the town of Lecompton did not adopt a single constitution and submit the proposal to a referendum for approval or rejection. Instead, the convention produced two documents and asked the voters of the territory to choose between a constitution "with slavery" and a constitution "without slavery." The difficulty was that although the "without slavery" version prohibited the further importation of slaves into Kansas, it also provided that the two hundred slaves already in the state would remain enslaved, as would their descendants. In addition, both versions of the constitution prohibited amendments to the slavery-related provisions for a period of seven years. For obvious reasons, these provisions were unacceptable to the antislavery forces in Kansas. They boycotted the December 21 referendum. As a result, the more extreme "with slavery" version of the constitution was approved by an overwhelming majority and sent to Congress for approval. Buchanan threw his support behind the Lecompton constitution and on February 2, 1858, submitted it to both houses of Congress together with a message urging the admission of Kansas under its provisions.

Predictably, Southern Democrats vigorously supported Buchanan. They argued that the logic of the doctrine of popular sovereignty required the admission of Kansas. Brushing aside the clear evidence that a majority of Kansans in fact opposed slavery, Southerners emphasized the formal legality of the process by which the constitution had been adopted. Thus, Sen. Albert G. Brown of Mississippi asked, "What becomes of this boasted doctrine that the people are allowed, in the name of popular sovereignty, to organize their domestic affairs in their own way, if you are to interpose at every point to tell them what they shall and shall not do and not only what they shall do, but how they shall do it?" Distinguishing popular sovereignty from populous sovereignty, Sen. James G. Hammond of South Carolina added that the relevant action was that "of a legal, constitutional ballot box. . . . The voice of the people is the voice of God; but when it is outside of that, it is the voice of a demon, the doctrine of the reign of terror."

Other Southern voices suggested that precisely because the foothold of slavery in Kansas was so tenuous, distaste for the process by which the Lecompton constitution had been adopted did not explain the fervor of the opposition. Sen. R. M. T. Hunter of Virginia asserted that opponents must either "desire to keep the question open for political purposes, or else because they are unwilling to admit, even for a moment, any State which tolerates slavery by its Constitution." Similarly, noting that virtually everyone understood that slavery was destined for early extinction in Kansas, the *Richmond Enquirer* declared that what was really at stake was "the great principle of equality."

Northern Democrats were divided. Some, like Sen. William Bigler of Indiana, took the view that the admission of Kansas was the best hope of easing sectional tensions. Observing that "it is conceded on all hands that Kansas is [eventually] to be a free state" and arguing that "the proceedings in her case were . . . more regular, legal and binding than in most cases," Bigler asserted that "the rejection of Kansas would tend to the perpetuity of this fruitless strife about slavery." Bigler's solution was to "let the two States of Kansas and Minnesota, come in, one slave and one free, as an exemplification of the compromises of 1850. . . . This will be wiser than the perpetuity of the war of crimination and recrimination, of assault on the one hand, repulse on the other."

Other free-state Democrats took a different view. They were led by Stephen Douglas himself, who described the process by which the Lecompton constitution was adopted as "a system of trickery and jugglery, designed to defeat the fair expression of the will of the people." Arguing that the principle of popular sovereignty required that the voters have an opportunity to consider all the provisions of a proposed state constitution rather than simply the issue of slavery, Douglas asserted that support for the admission of Kansas would require him "to forfeit my faith and my honor in order to enable a small minority of the people of Kansas to defraud a majority of that people out of their elective franchise."

Republicans, on the other hand, were completely united. To them, Buchanan's initiative was anathema. They denounced the effort to admit Kansas under the Lecompton constitution as further evidence of the influence of the slave power in American politics in general and the Democratic Party in particular. For example, Sen. Henry Wilson of Massachusetts described Buchanan's message as "a complete and absolute surrender by the President of the United States to the principles, the doctrines, the policy, and the sentiments of the slaveholding propagandists of this country," and Rep. Preston King of New York asserted that Democratic support for the Lecompton constitution demonstrated that "the organization of the Democratic party has fallen irretrievably under the control of nullifiers and slave propagandists."

Not surprisingly, references to *Dred Scott* played an important role in this characterization. For example, Sen. John P. Hale of New Hampshire accused the supporters of the Lecompton constitution as "proposing to carry out this Dred Scott decision by forcing upon the people of Kansas a constitution against which they have remonstrated, and to which, there can be no shadow of doubt, a very large portion of them are opposed," and Sen. William H. Seward of New York characterized the decision as an example of "judicial usurpation [that] is more odious and intolerable than any other among the manifold practices of tyranny." Seward also focused on two of the major themes in the more general Republican assault on *Dred Scott*. First, he contended that, because the Court had first concluded that it lacked jurisdiction because free blacks were not citizens, the discussion of the constitutionality of the Missouri Compromise was dictum. Second, he characterized the decision as part of a larger slave-power conspiracy to defend slavery and the interests of the slave states, darkly adverting to "whisperings" between Chief Justice Taney and President Buchanan at Buchanan's inauguration and noting that the next day (the day before the decision in *Dred Scott* was announced), "without even exchanging their silken robes for courtiers' gowns," the justices had visited Buchanan at the White House. Not surprisingly, such attacks engendered equally vigorous defenses of the merits of the *Dred Scott* decision by Southern Democrats, at times accompanied by denunciations of what Sen. Judah Benjamin of Louisiana described as the "violence [and] recklessness" of some of the charges levied against Taney and his compatriots by some Republicans.

Despite such exchanges, *Dred Scott* does not seem to have played a central role in the dispute over the admission of Kansas. In many ways the conflict was a reprise of the struggle over the passage of the Kansas-Nebraska Act four years earlier, with a quite different outcome. In the Senate, John J. Crittenden of Kentucky, a member of the American Party, which had attracted a substantial number of former Whigs, proposed to submit the Lecompton constitution to a straight up-or-down vote by the people of Kansas. This proposal failed on a 34-24 vote. The original bill then passed the Senate on March 23 by a vote of 33-25, with four Northern Democrats and two Southern American Party members joining the united Republicans in opposition.

However, despite the efforts of President Buchanan, supporters of the Lecompton constitution proved unable to muster a majority in the House of Representatives, as nineteen to twenty-four Northern Democrats consistently joined members of the Republican and Know Nothing parties to create narrow majorities on crucial early procedural votes. On April 1 the House voted 120-112 to replace the Lecompton bill with a proposal identical to Crittenden's, which became known as the Crittenden-Montgomery amendment. The Senate refused to concur, and a conference committee was formed. On March 23 the committee reported a bill attributed to anti-Lecompton Democrat William H. English of Indiana that would have provided for the admission of Kansas as a state, provided that voters in the territory agreed to a reduction in the federal land grant that had been requested by the Lecompton convention. If the voters rejected the reduction, then Kansas would not become a state until its population was equal to that normally required for one representative in the House.

All parties to the controversy understood that antislavery voters in Kansas would seize on the referendum as an opportunity to prevent admission of Kansas as a slave state. Thus, in practical terms, the effect of the English proposal was much the same as that of the Crittenden-Montgomery amendment. Nonetheless, Southerners realized that the English proposal provided them with a chance to gain at least a symbolic recognition of the legitimacy of the Lecompton constitution — the most they could possibly achieve under the circumstances. Thus, in the House of Representatives and the Senate, the voting patterns on the two provisions were almost mirror images of one another. The exception was the anti-Lecompton Democrats, most of whom seized on the English proposal as an opportunity to prevent the admission of Kansas as a slave state while avoiding total repudiation of the Democratic administration. Their votes proved critical on April 30, when, after having been approved by the Senate by a vote of 31-22, the English bill passed the House on a vote of 112-103. As expected, on August 2 Kansas voters overwhelmingly rejected the reduction in the land grant, and Kansas remained out of the Union until it was admitted as a free state in 1861.

The passage of the English bill and the subsequent rejection of statehood in the August 2 referendum effectively removed the issue of Kansas as a sectional irritant. However, Northern Democrats paid a heavy political price for the effort to vindicate the Lecompton constitution. Whereas fifty-three free state Democrats had been elected to the House of Representatives in 1856, only thirty-two survived the election of 1858. The same election saw the contest for a Senate seat from Illinois between Stephen Douglas, who had joined Republicans in opposing the English bill, and Abraham Lincoln. *Dred Scott* played an important role in the series of memorable debates between the two candidates that marked that contest.

Well before the debates began, Douglas had made his views on *Dred Scott* crystal clear. He outlined those views at length on June 12, 1857, in a major speech in Springfield, Illinois. In that speech he enunciated what Fehrenbacher has described as the doctrine of "residual popular sovereignty." While conceding that *Dred Scott* established the right of Southerners to bring slaves into the federal territories without congressional interference, Douglas also declared that "it necessarily remains a barren and a worthless right, unless sustained, protected and enforced by appropriate police regulations and local legislation, prescribing adequate remedies for its violation. These regulations and remedies must necessarily depend entirely upon the will and wishes of the people of the Territory, as they can only be prescribed by the local Legislatures. Hence, the great principle of popular sovereignty and self-government is sustained and firmly established by the authority of [*Dred Scott*]." In addition, Douglas lavishly praised the holding that free blacks could not be citizens of the United States, asserting that the framers of the Constitution had understood the Declaration of Independence as applying only to whites and echoing Taney's assertion that in the late eighteenth century, black people had universally been regarded as inferior beings.

The latter view formed the basis for Douglas's attacks on Lincoln's reaction to *Dred Scott*. Noting that Lincoln had challenged Taney's conclusion that the descendants of slaves could not be citizens of the United States, Douglas declared, "I do not believe that the almighty ever intended the negro to be the equal of the white man" and "I am opposed to negro citizenship in any and every form." He also said, "If you desire negro citizenship, if you desire to allow them to come into the State and settle with the white man, if you desire them to vote on an equality with yourselves, and to make them eligible to office, to serve on juries, and to adjudge your rights, then support Mr. Lincoln and the Black Republican party."

This assault created something of a dilemma for Lincoln. On one hand, to be viewed as being in favor of "negro equality" was a substantial political liability in the racist American society of the antebellum era — particularly in a state such as Illinois, which had gone so far as to outlaw the immigration of free blacks. On the other hand, accepting Taney's analysis of the citizenship issue might soften the force of Lincoln's critique of *Dred Scott* as a whole. Faced with this problem, Lincoln temporized. While declaring himself personally opposed to granting citizenship to free blacks, Lincoln argued that Taney had taken the wrong approach to the citizenship issue because the Chief Justice had applied a national standard on the citizenship issue rather than allowing each state to decide for itself whether resident free blacks could be considered citizens.

Lincoln made a quite different use of *Dred Scott* in his attack on Douglas. The core of this attack was the claim that "the introduction of the Nebraska bill into Congress [by Douglas] was [part of] a conspiracy to make slavery perpetual and national," that "we see a lot of framed timbers, different portions of which we know have been gotten out by different workmen — Stephen [Douglas], Franklin [Pierce], Roger [Brooke Taney] and James [Buchanan] . . . and when we see they make exactly make the frame of a house or a mill, all the tenons and mortices exactly fitting . . . we feel it impossible not to believe that Stephen and Franklin, and Roger and James, all understood one another from the beginning, and all worked upon a common plan or draft drawn before the first blow was struck." While conceding that Douglas may not have specifically discussed *Dred Scott* with either Buchanan or Taney, Lincoln suggested that Douglas "had as perfect an understanding [of the conspiracy] without talking as with it."

Throughout the debates, Lincoln also asserted that the Supreme Court had not completed its role in the slave-power conspiracy with the decision in *Dred Scott*. He predicted darkly that, having proclaimed in *Dred Scott* that slavery was a constitutionally protected species of property, the Court would next hold it unconstitutional for any *state* to outlaw slavery within its borders. This indeed had been the view of *Dred Scott* taken in an article published on November 17, 1857, in the *Washington Union* — the official organ of the Buchanan administration. Although this view was far more extreme than the views expressed by most supporters of *Dred Scott*, its expression in such a prominent Democratic publication gave some credence to Lincoln's claim that Taney's opinion was merely an intermediate step toward the full nationalization of slavery.

The specter of a vast slave-power conspiracy provided the backdrop for the famous exchange between Lincoln and Douglas during the debate at Freeport, Illinois, on August 27, 1858. Lincoln posed four specific questions to Douglas during that debate, two of which related directly to the implications of *Dred Scott*. In question 2, Lincoln asked, "Can the people of a United States Territory, in any lawful way, against the wish of any citizen of the United States, exclude slavery from its limits prior to the formation of a State Constitution?" Drawing upon the slave-power conspiracy theory, in question 3 he asked, "If the Supreme Court of the United States shall decide that States cannot exclude slavery from their limits, are you in favor of acquiescing in, adopting and following such decision as a rule of political action?" In answering question 2, Douglas reiterated the position he had taken in Springfield in May 1857. However, he refused to answer question 3 directly. Noting that even Southerners had condemned the *Washington Union* article, Douglas declared that "there never was but one man in America, claiming any degree of intelligence or decency, who ever for a moment pretended such a thing," and that "[Lincoln] casts an imputation upon the Supreme Court, by supposing that they would violate the Constitution of the United States. . . . It would be an act of treason that no man on the bench could ever descend to." These answers helped preserve Douglas's seat in the Senate. Although Republicans actually received a majority of the votes cast in the elections for the state legislature, Democrats won control of a majority of the seats in both houses of the legislature. Thus, they were able to reelect Douglas.

Nationally, many Democratic Party leaders — particularly those in the South — were not enamored with Douglas's response to *Dred Scott*. The dispute over the admission of Kansas under the Lecompton constitution both alienated Southern Democrats from Douglas and hardened Southern positions still further on the basic issue of slavery in the territories, leaving them unwilling to accept any limiting interpretation of *Dred Scott*. Thus, when Sen. Jefferson Davis of Mississippi suggested on September 11, 1857, that he agreed with the doctrine of residual popular sovereignty (which has become known as the Freeport Doctrine), heavy criticism from Democrats in his home state quickly forced him to retreat. Southerners and their allies became even more alarmed in 1859 when the Kansas territorial legislature, now controlled by antislavery forces, enacted a bill that would have outlawed slavery in the territory. Although the bill was pocket-vetoed by the governor, it dramatized the fact that the Freeport Doctrine was indeed a serious threat to Southern interests and a potential threat to the theoretical gains made by proslavery forces in *Dred Scott.*

Equally importantly, the more general failure of the antislavery forces to retreat in the face of an authoritative decision rendered by the Supreme Court fueled the Southern conviction that Northerners were determined to run roughshod over protections that Southerners believed were provided to them by the Constitution. For example, on January 6, 1860, the *Richmond Semi-Weekly Examiner* declared that "the refusal of the majority [in the North] to recognize the decision of the Supreme Court in the Dred Scott case as law . . . prove[s] the inefficiency of legal, judicial or constitutional defenses against the encroachments of majorities who hold physical power." Against this background, Southerners increasingly viewed the doctrine of nonintervention as insufficient to protect their interests. Instead, Southerners such as Davis and Sen. Albert Gallatin Brown of Mississippi pressed for congressional adoption of a slave code that would explicitly recognize the right of slaveowners to bring slaves into the territories.

The dispute over the Freeport Doctrine and the candidacy of Douglas led to the disruption of the Democratic Party when party representatives met to choose a presidential candidate at the national convention that opened in Charleston, South Carolina, on April 23, 1860. Southern delegates, who controlled the platform committee, pressed for a plank that would have declared that "it is the duty of the Federal Government . . . to protect, when necessary, the rights of persons and property in the territories" — a thinly veiled call for the adoption of a slave code by Congress. However, the Douglas forces, who had a bare majority of the delegates to the convention as a whole, succeeded in replacing this provision with language recognizing the difference of opinion among Democrats on the issue of the power of the territorial legislatures to ban slavery and declaring that "the Democratic party will abide by the decision of the Supreme Court of the United States upon these questions of Constitutional Law." Rather than accept this plank, all of the delegates from the lower South formally withdrew from the convention. Because of the two-thirds rule, even after their withdrawal Douglas was unable to muster the number of votes necessary to claim the nomination. On May 3 the delegates voted to adjourn and resume their deliberations in Baltimore on June 18. In Baltimore a majority voted to seat pro-Douglas delegations from a number of the states that had bolted from the Charleston convention, and these delegations provided the necessary votes to nominate Douglas. The Southern dissidents responded by nominating Sen. John Breckenridge of Kentucky on the proslavery platform that had been rejected in Charleston.

In addition to alienating Southern Democrats, the equivocation regarding the platform on slavery in the territories left Douglas vulnerable to attacks from Republican candidate Abraham Lincoln in the general election. From the beginning, with no hope of competing in the South in any event, the strategy of the Republicans was to paint Douglas as a tool of the slave-power conspiracy. Republicans pointedly noted that in *Dred Scott*, Taney had asserted that territorial legislatures lacked the authority to ban slavery. Similarly, on December 17, 1859, in his third annual message, President Buchanan declared that the Court had held that slaveowners had the right to bring slaves into the territories and that "neither Congress *nor a Territorial legislature* has any authority to annul or impair this sacred right" (emphasis added). Thus, Republicans argued, by pledging fealty to a decision of the Supreme Court on the question of the power of territorial legislatures, Douglas had effectively abandoned the Freeport Doctrine and embraced a view that was functionally no different than that of the most proslavery elements of the Democratic Party. This charge was an important element in the message that allowed Lincoln to win every important nonslave state and claim the presidency.

In theory, the election of Lincoln might have been the precursor to a confrontation with the Court over the issue of slavery in the territories. Throughout the campaign, Lincoln consistently maintained that, as president, he would not feel bound to follow the dictates of the *Dred Scott* decision because he had not been a party to the suit. He reiterated this point in his first inaugural address. While denying that he was launching "any assault on the [Supreme] court or the judges," Lincoln declared that

> I do not forget the position, assumed by some, that constitutional questions are to be decided by the Supreme Court; nor do I deny that such decisions must be binding in any case, upon the parties

to a suit; as to the object of that suit, while they are also entitled to very high respect and consideration in all parallel cases by all other departments of the government, . . . At the same time, the candid citizen must confess that if the policy of the government upon vital questions, affecting the whole people is to be irrevocably fixed by decisions of the Supreme Court, the instant they are made . . . the people will have ceased to be their own rulers having to that extent practically resigned their government into the hands of that eminent tribunal.

Of course, the potential confrontation between Lincoln and the Court over the holding in *Dred Scott* never materialized. Instead, the election of 1860 triggered a far more serious constitutional crisis. Unwilling to remain associated with a federal government dominated by the Republican Party, most of the slave states seceded, and Lincoln responded by launching a military campaign to compel the seceding states to remain in the Union. Modern historians generally do not view *Dred Scott* as a major cause of the Civil War; however, the war clearly led to the demise of the constitutional doctrines embraced by Chief Justice Taney and the other members of the majority of the Court.

CHAPTER 10

Dred Scott and the Limits of Judicial Power

The justices who formed the majority in *Dred Scott* clearly misapprehended the impact their decision would have on the political disputes that were wracking the country in 1857. Chief Justice Taney and his cohorts hoped the decision would at once spike the guns of the Republican Party and also help ease sectional tensions by providing a final settlement to the long-running dispute over slavery in the territories. In fact, the decision had precisely the opposite effect. It bolstered Republican claims that the Democratic Party was in fact the tool of a vast slave-power conspiracy, was a factor in the ultimate disruption of the Democratic Party itself, and even played a role in moving the Republican Party toward acceptance of the concept of African American citizenship.

The miscalculation by the members of the *Dred Scott* majority reflected an overestimation of the power of the Court in the American political system. In the ordinary run of cases — even constitutional cases — the parties, the public, and even other political actors will generally accept the doctrines laid down by the Court and conform their actions even to those doctrines with which they disagree. However, when the Court attempts to resolve fundamental political differences, particularly in situations where the battle lines are already clearly drawn, the dynamic changes. Those whose positions are threatened by the Court's action are unlikely to simply acquiesce and abandon their views. Instead, they will attack the decision of the Court and continue the struggle in other venues. The Court's decision might become a focal point of the struggle and even have some practical impact. However, in the long run, it is control of the other branches of government rather than the Court that will determine the outcome.

The aftermath of *Dred Scott* dramatically illustrates this point. For the leaders of the Republican Party, acquiescence in the result would have been political suicide; they had no choice but to attack the decision and, when possible, turn it into a positive by citing it as an example of the strength of the slave-power conspiracy. Within four years they were successful in seizing the reins of power in the federal government by electing Lincoln to the presidency. Even if the Southern states had not seceded after the election of 1860, it is difficult to imagine the doctrines embraced by the *Dred Scott* majority surviving four years of Republican rule.

Ultimately, then, the story of *Dred Scott* is a story of judicial hubris. Taney's approach to the issues of slavery in the territories and the status of free blacks not only are abhorrent in substance. They also reflect a fundamental misunderstanding of the appropriate role of the Supreme Court in the American political system. No judge today would agree with Taney regarding the substance of *Dred Scott*. Those who embrace his vision of the judicial function do so only at their peril.

CHRONOLOGY

1787   Adoption of Northwest Ordinance, prohibiting slavery in federally held territories north of the Ohio River. Adoption of the Constitution by the Philadelphia Convention, including the three-fifths clause, fugitive slave clause, and slave trade clause.

1789   Ratification of the Constitution.

1790   Adoption of the Southwest Ordinance, organizing federally held territories south of the Ohio River with no prohibition on slavery.

1800   Thomas Jefferson defeats John Adams for the presidency, in part because of the three-fifths clause.

1803   The United States purchases Louisiana from France.

1804   The Senate defeats a proposal to outlaw slavery in the territory acquired in the Louisiana Purchase.

1819   Missouri petitions Congress to be allowed to adopt a constitution and form a state government. The United States renounces its claims to Texas in the Adams-Onis Treaty.

1820   The adoption of the Missouri Compromise allows Missouri to form a constitution that allows slavery; forbids slavery in all other areas of the Louisiana Purchase north of 36 degrees, 30 minutes; and admits Maine as a free state.

1821   Missouri admitted as a slave state.

1825   The Supreme Court decides *The Antelope*.

1827   The United States and Great Britain agree to joint occupation of the Oregon Territory.

1829   John McLean appointed to the U.S. Supreme Court.

1833   Dred Scott sold to Dr. John Emerson.

1833–1836   John Emerson and Dred Scott reside at Fort Armstrong in the state of Illinois.

1835   James Moore Wayne appointed to the U.S. Supreme Court.

1836   Texas declares its independence from Mexico. The Missouri Supreme Court rejects the doctrine of reattachment in *Rachel v. Walker*. Roger Brooke Taney appointed chief justice of the U.S. Supreme Court.

1836–1837	John Emerson and Dred Scott reside at Fort Snelling in Wisconsin Territory. Dred Scott marries Harriet.
1837	John Catron appointed to the U.S. Supreme Court.
1838	Eliza Scott born on board the *Gipsey*, north of the Missouri Compromise line.
1841	The Supreme Court decides *Groves v. Slaughter* and *United States v. The Amistad*. Peter V. Daniel appointed to the U.S. Supreme Court.
1842	The Supreme Court decides *Prigg v. Pennsylvania*, clarifying the respective roles of the state and federal governments in dealing with fugitive slaves.
1843	John Scott dies.
1844	Treaty providing for annexation of Texas defeated in the Senate. James K. Polk elected president on a platform advocating the annexation of Texas and that the United States demand possession of the entire Oregon Territory.
1845	Samuel Nelson appointed to the U.S. Supreme Court.
1846	The United States declares war on Mexico. The United States and Great Britain agree on a treaty dividing Oregon at the forty-ninth parallel. The Wilmot Proviso, which would have barred slavery from any territory ceded by Mexico, is introduced in Congress but does not pass. Dred Scott and his family file suits for freedom in Missouri state court but lose in trial court on a technicality. Robert C. Grier appointed to the U.S. Supreme Court.
1847	New trial granted in the Scotts' suit for freedom.
1848	Under the Treaty of Guadalupe Hidalgo, which ends the Mexican War, the United States obtains the territory west of Texas and south of the Oregon Territory. Slavery is barred from the Oregon Territory.
1849	California submits a proposed constitution barring slavery and petitions Congress to be admitted as a state.
1850	Verdict and judgment for the Scotts in Missouri trial court. Congress passes the Compromise of 1850, admitting California as a free state, organizing Utah and New Mexico Territories on the basis of popular sovereignty, and strengthening the Fugitive Slave Law.
1851	The Supreme Court decides *Strader v. Graham*, holding that slave states are free to apply the doctrine of reattachment to

slaves whose masters voluntarily allowed them to spend time in states where they became free by law. Benjamin Robbins Curtis appointed to the U.S. Supreme Court.

1852	The Missouri Supreme Court reverses the trial court judgment and holds that the Scotts remain slaves.
1853	The Kansas-Nebraska Act repeals the Missouri Compromise and organizes the Kansas and Nebraska territories on the basis of popular sovereignty. *Dred Scott v. Sandford* filed in U.S. Circuit Court. John Campbell appointed to the U.S. Supreme Court.
1853–1856	Struggle between proslavery and antislavery forces in Kansas. Demise of the Whig Party and rise of the Republican Party.
1854	Circuit court holds that the Scotts remain slaves. The Scotts appeal to the U.S. Supreme Court.
1856	The Supreme Court twice hears arguments in *Dred Scott*.
1857	The Supreme Court announces its decision in *Dred Scott*. Curtis resigns from the Court after dispute with Taney over publication of *Dred Scott* opinions. The Lecompton constitution drafted by a convention in Kansas and approved in a referendum boycotted by antislavery forces.
1858	Congress rejects the Lecompton constitution. The Lincoln-Douglas debates focus on *Dred Scott*.
1860	Disruption of Democratic Party and election of Lincoln as president.
1865	Ratification of the Thirteenth Amendment.
1868	Ratification of the Fourteenth Amendment.

BIBLIOGRAPHIC ESSAY

Note from the series editors: The following bibliographic essay contains the primary and secondary sources that the author consulted for this volume. We have asked all authors in the series to omit formal citations in order to make our volumes more readable, inexpensive, and appealing for students and general readers. In adopting this format, Landmark Law Cases and American Society follows the precedent of a number of highly regarded and widely consulted series.

The account of *Dred Scott* in this book is based on a variety of both primary and secondary sources. The opinions in the case itself are reproduced in *United States Reports*, as are the opinions in the other slavery-related Supreme Court cases discussed in the book. The briefs filed in the case and the text of the arguments of Montgomery Blair and George Ticknor Curtis can be found in Paul Finkelman, ed., *Slavery, Race, and the American Legal System, 1700–1872*, 16 vols. (New York: Garland Publishing Co., 1988), vol. 3, pp. 17–179. The opinions in *Scott v. Emerson* can be found in *Missouri Reports*, and the state court decision in *Strader v. Graham* is readily available in *B. Munroe Reports*, which collects the decisions of the Kentucky Supreme Court for the relevant period.

Unfortunately, the lower-court proceedings in *Dred Scott* are not available in published form. The official records of the case can be examined in the archives of the U.S. district court for the Eastern District of Missouri. The correspondence between Roswell Field and Montgomery Blair is preserved in the Dred Scott Collection, maintained by the Missouri Historical Society.

The indispensable source for understanding the evolution of the political dispute over slavery in the territories is the debates in Congress, which are compiled in the *Annals of Congress* and the *Congressional Globe*. The debates over the three-fifths clause and other slavery-related provisions in the Constitution can be found in Max Farrand, ed., *The Records of the Federal Convention of 1787*, 4 vols., rev. ed. (New Haven, Conn.: Yale University Press, 1937), and Bernard Bailyn, ed., *The Debate on the Constitution: Federalist and Antifederalist Speeches, Articles, and Letters During the Struggle over Ratification*, 2 vols. (New York: Viking Press, 1983).

Contemporary newspapers provided differing perspectives on the disputes over slavery. For example, the *New York Daily Tribune* reflected the antislavery viewpoint, the *Charleston Mercury* gave the extreme Southern viewpoint, and the *Washington Union* was the official organ of the Buchanan administration. In addition, newspapers such as the *Tribune*, the *New York Times*, and the Philadelphia *North American and United States Gazette* gave detailed accounts of the oral arguments before the Supreme Court in *Dred Scott*.

Dred Scott is also the subject of a vast secondary literature, including a number of fine monographs focusing specifically on various aspects of the decision. Don E. Fehrenbacher, *The Dred Scott Case: Its Significance in American Law and Politics* (New York: Oxford University Press, 1978) is the indispensable starting point for any student of the case. Walter Ehrlich, *They Have No Rights: Dred Scott's Struggle for Freedom* (Westport, Conn.: Greenwood Press, 1979) is particularly good regarding the details of the litigation. Paul Finkelman, Dred Scott v. Sandford: *A Brief History with Documents* (New York: St. Martin's Press, 1997) reproduces selections from primary sources. Among older studies, Vincent C. Hopkins, *Dred Scott's Case* (New York: Russell and Russell Publishers, 1967) remains useful.

Carl B. Swisher, *History of the Supreme Court: Volume V, The Taney Period* (New York: Macmillan Publishing Co., 1972), provides a comprehensive discussion of the Supreme Court's slavery-related jurisprudence from *Groves v. Slaughter* through *Prigg*, as does the older Charles Warren, *The Supreme Court in United States History*, 2 vols., rev. ed. (Boston: Little Brown, 1932), vol. 2. Harold M. Hyman and William M. Wiecek, *Equal Justice Under Law: Constitutional Development, 1835–1875* (New York: Harper and Row, 1982), cover much of the same material from a different perspective, as does William M. Wiecek, "Slavery and Abolition Before the United States Supreme Court, 1820–1860," *Journal of American History* 65 (1978): 34–59.

Don E. Fehrenbacher and Ward M. McAfee, *The Slaveholding Republic: An Account of the United States Government's Relations to Slavery* (New York: Oxford University Press, 2002), comprehensively examine the impact of slavery on the political decisions of the antebellum era. Michael Morrison, *Slavery and the American West: The Eclipse of Manifest Destiny and the Coming of the Civil War* (Chapel Hill: University of North Carolina Press, 1997), provides a detailed, balanced account of the political struggle over slavery in the territories. Major L. Wilson, *Space, Time, and Freedom: The Quest for Nationality and the Irrepressible Conflict* (Westport, Conn.: Greenwood Press, 1974), is also extremely helpful, as is Peter B. Knupfer, *The Union as It Is: Constitutional Unionism and Sectional Compromise, 1787–1861* (Chapel Hill: University of North Carolina Press, 1991). Leonard L. Richards, *The Slave Power: The Free North and Southern Domination, 1780–1860* (Baton Rouge: Louisiana University Press, 2000), chronicles the dispute from the point of view of Northern Democrats and argues that the conflict was rooted in unreasonable demands by the South. Conversely, William J. Cooper Jr., *Liberty and Slavery: Southern Politics to 1860* (New York: Alfred A. Knopf, 1983), and *The South and the Politics of Slavery, 1828–1856* (Baton Rouge: Louisiana State University Press, 1978), tells the story from the Southern perspective, as does William W. Freehling, *The Road to Disunion, Volume I: Secessionists at Bay, 1776–1854* (New York: Oxford University Press, 1990), although the latter two books unfortunately end just before the *Dred Scott* decision itself.

David Potter's *The Impending Crisis: 1848–1861* (New York: Harper and Row, 1976) is the consensus choice as the best history of the events from the Wilmot Proviso to the secession of the Southern states. Allan Nevins's *The Emergence of Lincoln*, 2 vols. (New York: Charles Scribner's Sons, 1950) is also a classic. In addition, see Richard H. Sewell, *Sectionalism and Civil War, 1848–1865* (Baltimore, Md.: Johns Hopkins University Press, 1988), and Michael F. Holt, *The Fate of Their Country: Politicians, Slavery Extension, and the Coming of the Civil War* (New York: Farrar, Straus and Giroux, 2005).

In addition to these wide-ranging studies, I drew on a variety of scholarly works that dealt with the specific political and jurisprudential issues covered in the book. Donald L. Robinson, *Slavery in the Structure of American Politics, 1763–1820* (New York: Harcourt Brace Jovanovich, 1971), provides a comprehensive treatment of all of the issues covered in Chapter 2. For differing perspectives on the prohibition of slavery in the Northwest Ordinance, see David Brion Davis, "The Significance of Excluding Slavery from the Old Northwest in 1787," *Indiana Magazine of History* 84 (1988): 75–89; Paul Finkelman, "Slavery and the Northwest Ordinance: A Study in Ambiguity," *Journal of the Early Republic* 6 (1986): 343–370, and Staughton Lynd, "The Compromise of 1787," in *Class Conflict, Slavery, and the United States Constitution* (Westport, Conn.: Greenwood Press, 1980), pp. 185–213. Peter Onuf, *Statehood and Union: A History of the Northwest Ordinance* (Indianapolis: Indiana University Press, 1987), places the issue of slavery in the context of the evolution of the Northwest Ordinance more generally. Paul Finkelman, "Evading the Ordinance: The Persistence of Bondage in Indiana and Illinois," *Journal of the Early Republic* 9 (1989): 21–51, demonstrates that in the absence of the prohibition adopted in 1787, slavery would have taken hold permanently in the Old Northwest.

Paul Finkelman, "Slavery and the Constitutional Convention: Making a Covenant with Death," in Richard Beeman, Stephen Botein, and Edward C. Carter II, eds., *Beyond Confederation: Origins of the Constitution and American National Identity* (Chapel Hill: University of North Carolina Press, 1987), pp. 188–255; William M. Wiecek, "The Witch at the Christening: Slavery and the Constitution's Origins," in Leonard Levy, ed., *The Framing and Ratification of the Constitution* (New York: The Free Press, 1987), pp. 167–184; and Garry Wills, *"Negro President": Jefferson and the Slave Power* (Boston: Houghton Mifflin Co., 2003), pp. 50–61, argue that the three-fifths clause was a major concession to the South. Earl M. Maltz, "The Idea of the Pro-Slavery Constitution," *Journal of the Early Republic* 17 (1997): 37–59, and Harold A. Ohline, "Republicanism and Slavery: Origins of the Three-Fifths Clause in the United States Constitution," *William and Mary Quarterly* (1971): 563–584, view the same clause as a reasonable compromise. Wills emphasizes the significance of the three-fifths clause to Jefferson's victory in the presidential election of 1800.

Stanley M. Elkins and Eric L. McKitrick, *The Age of Federalism* (New York: Oxford University Press, 1997), p. 457, conclude that Jefferson would have won the election in any event if it had been decided by a popular vote.

Glover Moore's *The Missouri Controversy: 1819–1821* (Lexington: University of Kentucky Press, 1953) is the standard source on the enactment of the Missouri Compromise. Don E. Fehrenbacher, *The South and Three Sectional Crises: Friends, Foes, and Reform* (Baton Rouge: Louisiana State University Press, 1980), pp. 9–25, provides additional insights.

R. Kent Newmyer, *Supreme Court Justice Joseph Story: Statesman of the Old Republic* (Chapel Hill: University of North Carolina Press, 1985), ch. 10, gives accounts of each of the cases discussed in Chapter 3. John T. Noonan, *Antelope: The Ordeal of the Captured Africans in the Administrations of John Quincy Adams and James Monroe* (Berkeley: University of California Press, 1990), explores *The Antelope* in detail. G. Edward White, *History of the Supreme Court of the United States: The Marshall Court and Cultural Change, 1815–35* (New York: Macmillan Publishing Co., 1988), pp. 693–703, is also useful. David Lightner, "The Supreme Court and the Interstate Slave Trade: A Study in Evasion, Anarchy and Extremism," *Journal of Supreme Court History* 29 (November 2004): 229–253, gives a good account of *Groves v. Slaughter*.

The Amistad is the subject of an enormous secondary literature. Howard Jones, *Mutiny on the Amistad: The Saga of a Slave Revolt and Its Impact on American Abolition, Law, and Diplomacy* (New York: Oxford University Press, 1987), is an excellent place to start.

Surprisingly, *Prigg v. Pennsylvania* has not been the subject of a book-length treatment. However, Paul Finkelman has produced a trilogy of important articles on the case: *"Prigg v. Pennsylvania:* Understanding Justice Story's Pro-Slavery Nationalism," *Journal of Supreme Court History* 2 (1997): 51–64; "Story-Telling on the Supreme Court: *Prigg v. Pennsylvania* and Justice Joseph Story's Judicial Nationalism," *Supreme Court Review* (1994): 247–294; and "Sorting out *Prigg v. Pennsylvania*," *Rutgers Law Journal* 24 (1993): 605–666. Finkelman argues that *Prigg* was a decisive victory for the South. A number of other commentators take a similar view: Fehrenbacher and McAfee, *The Slaveholding Republic*, p. 221; Newmyer, *Supreme Court Justice Joseph Story*, p. 370; and Barbara Holden-Smith, "Lords of the Lash, Loom, and Law: Justice Joseph Story, Slavery, and *Prigg v. Pennsylvania*," *Cornell Law Review* 78 (1993): 1086–1151. For other perspectives, see Thomas D. Morris, *Free Men All: The Personal Liberty Laws of the North* (Baltimore, Md.: Johns Hopkins University Press, 1974), pp. 94–105; Christopher L. M. Eisgruber, "Comment: Joseph Story, Slavery, and the Natural Law Foundations of American Constitutionalism," *University of Chicago Law Review* 55 (1988): 273–327; and Earl M. Maltz, "Majority, Concurrence and Dissent: *Prigg v. Pennsylvania* and the Structure of Supreme Court Decisionmaking," *Rutgers Law Journal* 31 (1999): 345–398.

Newmyer, *Chief Justice Joseph Story*, pp. 374–375, and Joseph C. Burke, "What Did the *Prigg* Case Really Decide?" *Pennsylvania Magazine of History and Biography* 93 (1969): 73–85, argue that the silence of Catron and McKinley in *Prigg* should not be taken to indicate that they agreed with Justice Story's analysis. However, as Finkelman observes in "Sorting Out *Prigg v. Pennsylvania*," a justice who does not note a disagreement with an opinion denominated as the "Opinion for the Court" is normally presumed to have joined fully in that opinion.

The annexation of Texas is discussed from various viewpoints in Thomas R. Hietala, *Manifest Design: Anxious Aggrandizement in Late Jacksonian America* (Ithaca, N.Y.: Cornell University Press, 1985), chs. 2 and 3; Frederick Merk, *Slavery and the Annexation of Texas* (New York: Alfred A. Knopf, 1972); David M. Pletcher, *The Diplomacy of Annexation: Texas, Oregon, and the Mexican War* (Columbia: University of Missouri Press, 1973); Charles G. Sellers, *James K. Polk, Continentalist, 1843–1846* (Princeton, N.J.: Princeton University Press, 1966); Joel H. Silbey, *Storm over Texas: The Annexation Controversy and the Road to Civil War* (New York: Oxford University Press, 2005); and Justin H. Smith, *The Annexation of Texas* (New York: AMS Press, 1971). The dispute over the Wilmot Proviso is the focus of Chaplain W. Morrison, *Democratic Politics and Sectionalism: The Wilmot Proviso Controversy* (Chapel Hill: University of North Carolina Press, 1967), and Eric Foner, "The Wilmot Proviso Revisited," *Journal of American History* 46 (1969): 262–279. In addition to the previously cited works of Pletcher and Sellers, Frederick Merk, *The Oregon Question: Essays in Anglo-American Diplomacy and Politics* (Cambridge, Mass.: Belknap Press: 1967), provides a detailed account of the background of the Oregon controversy; and R. Alton Lee, "Slavery and the Oregon Territorial Issue: Prelude to the Compromise of 1850," *Pacific Northwest Historical Quarterly* 44 (1973): 112–119, discusses the dispute over slavery in the Oregon Territory. For accounts of the Compromise of 1850, see Holden Hamilton, *Prologue to Conflict: The Crisis and Compromise of 1850* (Lexington: University of Kentucky Press, 1964), and John C. Waugh, *On the Brink of Civil War: The Compromise of 1850 and How It Changed the Course of American History* (Wilmington, Del.: Scholarly Resources, Inc., 2003).

The rise of the Republican Party is chronicled in Eric Foner, *Free Soil, Free Labor, Free Men: The Ideology of the Republican Party Before the Civil War* (New York: Oxford University Press, 1970); William E. Gienapp, *The Origins of the Republican Party, 1852–1856* (New York: Oxford University Press, 1987); and Michael F. Holt, *The Political Crisis of the 1850s* (New York: Wiley, 1978).

Paul Finkelman, *An Imperfect Union: Slavery, Federalism, and Comity* (Chapel Hill: University of North Carolina Press, 1981), provides a comprehensive examination of the case law dealing with the legal issues raised in *Dred Scott*. Robert R. Russel, "Constitutional Doctrines with Regard to Slavery in the Territories," *Journal of Southern History* 23 (1966): 466–488, summarizes the different constitutional positions on the issue of slavery in the territories. The different views expressed in political platforms can be found in Donald B. Johnson, ed., *National Party Platforms* (Champagne: University of Illinois Press, 1978). Arthur Bestor, "State Sovereignty and Slavery: A Reinterpretation of Proslavery Constitutional Doctrine, 1846–1860," *Journal of the Illinois State Historical Society* 54 (1961): 117–180, perceptively analyzes proslavery constitutional theory more generally. William M. Wiecek, "*Somerset:* Lord Mansfield and the Legitimacy of Slavery in the Anglo-American World," *University of Chicago Law Review* 42 (1974): 86–146, assesses the influence of *Somerset v. Stewart.* The discussion of the citizenship issue is taken from Earl M. Maltz, *The Fourteenth Amendment and the Law of the Constitution* (Durham, N.C.: Carolina Academic Press, 2003), pp. 40–42. Lea VanderVelde and Sandhya Subramanian, "Mrs. Dred Scott," *Yale Law Journal* 106 (1996): 1033–1122, speculate without direct evidence that Harriet Scott was the driving force behind the initial suit for freedom.

Biographical sketches of the justices who decided *Dred Scott* can be found in Swisher, *The Taney Court,* and Leon Friedman and Fred L. Israel, eds., *The Justices of the Supreme Court: Their Lives and Major Opinions,* 5 vols. (New York: Chelsea House, 1997). Taney is the subject of a number of full biographies, including H. H. Walker Lewis, *Without Fear or Favor: A Biography of Chief Justice Roger Brooke Taney* (Boston: Houghton Mifflin, 1965), and Carl B. Swisher, *Roger B. Taney* (New York: The Macmillan Co., 1935). John P. Frank's *Justice Daniel Dissenting: A Biography of Peter V. Daniel, 1784–1860* (Cambridge, Mass.: Augustus M. Kelley Publishers, 1964) is indispensable to any effort to understand Daniel's life and jurisprudence. Alexander A. Lawrence, *James Moore Wayne, Southern Unionist* (Chapel Hill: University of North Carolina Press, 1934) and *John Archibald Campbell: Southern Moderate* (Tuscaloosa: University of Alabama Press, 1997), provides useful information on Wayne and Campbell, respectively.

Francis P. Weisenburger's *The Life of John McLean: A Politician on the United States Supreme Court* (Columbus: Ohio State University Press, 1937) is the standard biography of McLean. Robert M. Cover, *Justice Accused: Antislavery and the Judicial Process* (New Haven, Conn.: Yale University Press, 1975), questions the depth of McLean's commitment to antislavery principles. Michael F. Holt, *The Rise and Fall of the American Whig Party: Jacksonian Politics and the Onset of the Civil War* (New York: Oxford University Press, 2003), pp. 261–272, 280–284, 290–297, explores McLean's efforts to gain the nomination of the Whig Party in 1848. Thomas E. Carney, "The Political Judge: Justice John McLean's Pursuit of the Presidency," *Ohio History* 111 (2002): 121–144, and Gienapp, *The Origins of the Republican Party,* pp. 311–316, 338–342, describe McLean's campaign for the Republican nomination in 1856.

Stuart Streichler, *Justice Curtis in the Civil War Era: At the Crossroads of American Constitutionalism* (Charlottesville: University of Virginia Press, 2005), examines Curtis's life and judicial philosophy, as does Richard H. Leach, "Benjamin R. Curtis: Case Study of a Supreme Court Justice," Ph.D. dissertation (Princeton University, 1951). Curtis's son gives his account of his father's life in Benjamin R. Curtis Jr., *A Memoir of Benjamin Robbins Curtis, with Some of his Professional and Miscellaneous Writings*, 2 vols. (Boston: Little, Brown and Co., 1879). The exchange of letters between Curtis and Taney regarding the release of opinions is reproduced in vol. 1, pp. 212–229. Curtis's views on slavery generally and *Dred Scott* in particular are also discussed in Earl M. Maltz, "The Unlikely Hero of *Dred Scott:* Benjamin Robbins Curtis and the Constitutional Law of Slavery," *Cardozo Law Review* 17 (1996): 1995–2016.

The impact of *Dred Scott* on the political landscape is described in Kenneth M. Stampp, *America in 1857: A Nation on the Brink* (New York: Oxford University Press, 2002), pp. 102–109. Mark E. Brandon, *Free in the World: American Slavery and Constitutional Failure* (Princeton, N.J.: Princeton University Press, 1988), situates the decision in the evolving struggle over the constitutional issues raised by slavery. The Lincoln-Douglas debates are compiled in Robert W. Johannsen, ed., *The Lincoln-Douglas Debates of 1858* (New York: Oxford University Press, 1965). Campaign literature from the presidential election of 1860 is collected in Joel H. Silbey, ed., *American Party Battle: Election Campaign Pamphlets, 1828–1876*, 2 vols. (Cambridge, Mass.: Harvard University Press, 1999), vol. 2, pp. 1854–1876. The text of Lincoln's first inaugural address can be found in William E. Gienapp, ed., *This Fiery Trial: The Speeches and Writings of Abraham Lincoln* (New York: Oxford University Press, 2002), pp. 57–66.

The evolution of the Thirteenth Amendment is chronicled in Michael Vorenberg, *Final Freedom: The Civil War, the Abolition of Slavery, and the Thirteenth Amendment* (New York: Cambridge University Press, 2001). Maltz, *The Fourteenth Amendment and the Law of the Constitution*, pp. 53–63, traces the development of the citizenship clause of the Fourteenth Amendment. On the drafting of the Fourteenth Amendment more generally, see Earl M. Maltz, *Civil Rights, the Constitution, and Congress, 1863–1869* (Lawrence: University Press of Kansas, 1990), and William E. Nelson, *The Fourteenth Amendment: From Political Principle to Judicial Doctrine* (Cambridge, Mass.: Harvard University Press, 1988).

McLean, John, *continued*
  presidential ambitions, 95–97,
    129–130
  view of slavery in territories, 94,
    130
Mexican Cession
  annexation, 1, 46
  border with Texas, 48–49, 50
  slavery issue, 47–49, 50, 51, 129
  Treaty of Guadalupe Hidalgo, 46
  Wilmot Proviso, 42–45, 47, 82,
    96
  See also California; New Mexico
Mexican War, 40, 42, 84
Mexico
  ban on slavery, 43, 51
  proposed treaties with, 42, 43
  Texas and, 35
  Treaty of Guadalupe Hidalgo, 46
Michigan
  comparison to Arkansas, 44
  statehood, 18
  state supreme court, 108
Miln. See *New York v. Miln*
Minnesota statehood, 146
Mississippi state constitution, 19,
    20, 21
Missouri
  Democratic Party, 68
  free blacks barred from, 15
  law on reattachment of slaves
    returning from free states, 67,
    124
  recognition of freedom of slaves
    emancipated in free states, 102
  state constitution, 15, 16
  See also Missouri statehood; Saint
    Louis
Missouri Compromise (1820), 2,
    14–18
  comparison to Compromise of
    1850, 50–51
  extension of line to Pacific, 46,
    47, 49, 90, 128
  Northern views of, 17
  as penal law, 70
  repeal by Kansas-Nebraska Act,
    54–57

restriction of slavery north of
    line, 14, 16
  Scott claims to freedom based on,
    112
  seen as repealed by Compromise
    of 1850, 53–54
  Southern acceptance, 46
Missouri Compromise (1820),
    constitutionality
  as issue in *Dred Scott,* 105, 106–
    107, 113–114, 116, 121–123,
    124, 125, 127–129, 130–131
  seen as unconstitutional, 46, 125,
    128, 129
Missouri statehood
  exclusion clause in constitution,
    15, 16
  slavery issue in debate, 4, 9–18
  Tallmadge amendment, 9–10,
    11–13
  See also Missouri Compromise
Missouri Supreme Court
  justices, 68–69
  Rachel v. Walker, 67, 69, 124
  See also *Dred Scott v. Emerson*
Monroe, James, 95
Morgan, Margaret, 29
Morris, Gouverneur, 22
Murdoch, Francis B., 63

Napton, William B., 68–69
Nashville Union and American,
    142–143
Nebraska Territory, 54–57
Negro Seamen's Acts, 72–73, 78,
    134
Nelson, Samuel
  appointment to Supreme Court,
    93
  background, 93–94
  Dred Scott deliberations, 107, 115,
    116
  opinion in *Dred Scott,* 123–124,
    131
New Mexico
  border with Texas, 48–49, 50
  cession to United States, 46
  statehood, 48